W9-BRE-336

·IRELAND·

AN ISLAND REVEALED

BARNES & NOBLE

TZGERALD'S

Text adapted from *Explorer Ireland* (AA Publishing) by Lindsay Hunt, with additional material by Molly McAnailly Burke.

This 2006 edition published by Barnes & Noble, Inc. by arrangement with AA Publishing (a trading name of Automobile Association Developments Limited, whose registered office is Fanum House, Basing View, Basingstoke, Hampshire RG21 4EA; registered number 1878835)

ISBN-13: 978-0-7607-8638-3
ISBN-10: 0-7607-8638-0

Printed and bound by C&C Offset, China

3 5 7 9 10 8 6 4 2

A03537

TITLE PAGE *Carrying a currach, Aran Islands*
PAGES 2–3 *Mist in the valley at Glendalough*
PAGES 4–5 *Avoca, near Wicklow*

CONTENTS

A. GUINNESS SON &

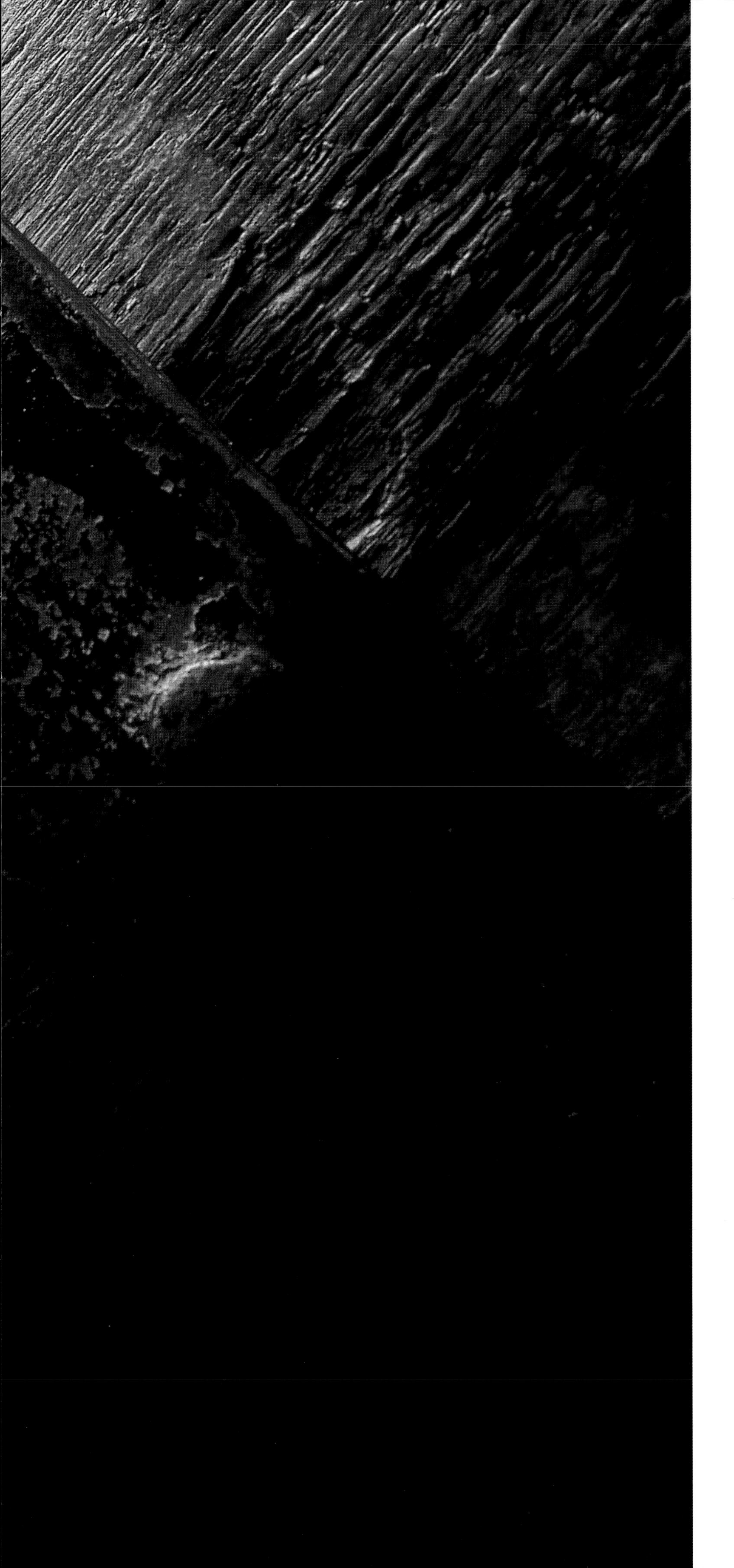

DUBLIN

This great city and its culture is changing at a rapid rate. Oscar Wilde claimed that 'life imitates art', and so Dublin today has traded on its cultural reputation to become a vibrant city of literary walks, rock music walks, pub tours and stars hanging out in the backrooms of nightclubs. Georgian, Victorian and Edwardian architecture were long associated with oppression here, and it is only now, as Dublin's massive youth population claim their rightful place as citizens of Europe, that bad memories, both real and traditional, are laid to rest and the city's architectural heritage reclaimed for the present. 'Dear dirty Dublin' is a thing of the past, and this is a city re-invented by James Joyce and U2, Roddy Doyle and 'Riverdance'.

You will still find old men in flat caps who claim to remember de Valera, and there are still talented traditional musicians playing for free in pubs. Guinness is still good for you, and you might still find a pub that won't serve pints to women. But the subtle change is that modern Dubliners have learned their worth on the world market, and a strategy for self-salesmanship has settled in for good. You had better get used to it.

The Guinness Brewery at St James's Gate has been a part of Dublin life for nearly 250 years

The City

The fair city? It is indeed a beautiful place, set on a broad river-basin fringed by the majestic sweep of Dublin Bay. Yet the 'fair city' of song was better described by James Joyce, one of its most famous citizens, as 'dear, dirty Dublin'. The best of its Georgian architecture rivals anything that can be seen in Bath or Edinburgh, but much has been destroyed by crass development or sheer neglect. Some of the demolition is forgivable; those pretty Georgian façades often disguised impossibly friable brickwork and tottering foundations that only total reconstruction would cure. Now, thankfully, the process is being reversed and Dublin's fanlit doorways glow amid newly restored surroundings.

To some extent, as in London, the great divide is the river. The Liffey neatly bisects Dublin from east to west, meeting the Poddle near the Grattan Bridge and forming the *dubh linn*, or dark pool, that gives the city its name. The respectable classes enjoy elegant architecture, smart restaurants and fashionable shops, now based mostly in the south around St Stephen's Green and Trinity College. In a few other areas the city's poor inhabit twilight zones where it is not recommended for tourists to stray.

Currently the Greater Dublin area contains about a million people, almost a third of the Republic's population, many of whom have drifted in from country areas in search of work. A large proportion of Dublin's inhabitants are under 25. It is a cosmopolitan city with many different nationalities and social groupings. Generally, there is a natural friendliness about both its citizens and the whole atmosphere of the city.

Dublin has declined since its 18th-century heyday, when great architecture sprouted all over the city, when the first performance of Handel's *Messiah* was held here, and when it was considered one of the foremost cities of Europe. Things have improved in recent years, however. A newfound prosperity and confidence inspires the Dublin scene: Georgian buildings and their contents are cherished and conserved, restaurants buzz with patrons, and many fashionable celebrities have made the city their second home.

Above: the magnificent 18th-century Custom House was designed by James Gandon

Right: the graceful span of Ha'penny Bridge links north and south Dublin

Left: the tall, narrow houses along Wellington Quay give the city a Continental air

SELECTED
SCOTCH POTATOES
SELECTED
SCOTCH POTATOES
SELECTED
SCOTCH POTATOES
THOMAS COURTNEY & SONS
LARGE

Georgian Dublin

East and west of O'Connell Street are densely crowded shopping areas, including the colorful open market of Moore Street, where you can be sure to get a tongue lashing in old Dublinese dialect if you dare squeeze the fruit or complain of being slipped a rotten one. The better off still shop on the south side's lively Grafton Street, stuffed with designer boutiques and malls, and beyond here you'll find some of the best preserved Georgian squares.

The period from 1714 to 1830 was Dublin's apogee, a great flowering of architecture, literature, philosophy and art. The quality of Irish craftsmanship in the superb Georgian buildings epitomises the 'age of elegance'. After the depredations of Cromwell's visits and the turmoil of Williamite battles, the 18th century was a time of comparative peace and prosperity here. Aesthetes and businessmen, wealthy gentry and talented artists merged resources to make Dublin one of the foremost cities of Europe. Terraces, parks, squares, imposing monuments and dignified town-houses burgeoned throughout the central parts of the city, bounded by the Grand and Royal canals. In 1757 the Wide Streets Commission, Europe's first planning authority, established new guidelines for development, and in 1773 the Paving Board set up regulations on lighting, cleaning and drainage, making densely populated residential areas much more salubrious.

The best examples of Georgian architecture can be seen south of the river. The city was largely spared during the World Wars, but fared ill at the hands of 20th-century developers and politicians. A new generation of conservation-minded citizens thankfully seem bent on preserving what is left.

Left: delivering essential supplies in the old way

Fine ironwork adorns the entrance to a magnificent Georgian terrace

Enjoy the details of Dublin architecture – these monkeys are to be found in Kildare Street

Trinity College

Entering the peaceful grounds of Trinity College, in the very heart of the city's traffic congestion, is like stepping into another world. This single-college university was founded by Elizabeth I in 1592 on confiscated monastery land, ostensibly 'to civilise Ireland with both learning and the Protestant religion'. Small wonder, then, that it became a source of division in the city. Catholics were always allowed entry to the college, and free education – provided of course they converted; up until 1966, Catholics had to obtain a special dispensation to attend on pain of excommunication. Now, however, the proportion of Catholic students at TCD, as it is known, is about 70 per cent. The roll of honour is impressive, including Edmund Burke, Jonathan Swift, Bram Stoker, Wolfe Tone, Oscar Wilde and Samuel Beckett.

Today TCD occupies a prime location at the heart of Dublin, in an oasis of gardens and parks. Inside, its buildings are arranged around quadrangles of lawns and cobbles. The theatre, examination hall, chapel, dining hall, and the old brick accommodation blocks known as the Rubrics can be seen as you pass from the Front Court to the Library Court.

To the right is the Old Library, which houses about 2 million volumes, stacked in a double-decker layer of huge - floor-to-ceiling shelving in 20 bays of a splendid cathedral-like hall, measuring 64m by 12m. The building was designed by Thomas Burgh in 1712; its barrel-vaulted ceiling was added in the 19th century. By far the most famous and precious of all the treasures here is the 8th-century illuminated manuscript of the four Gospels known as the *Book of Kells*. Inscribed in Latin on vellum parchment, its pages are magnificently ornamented with patterns and fantastic animals. Although the manuscript was certainly kept at the monastery of Kells in County Meath, there exists some doubt about whether it was actually produced there, some authorities believing it may have been copied in Iona or Lindisfarne.

Right: the tranquil courtyard of Trinity College is a world away from the bustle outside

With its high barrel roof and hushed air, Trinity College Library is like some extraordinary cathedral

Right: coffee houses are an important part of city life, whether cosy and traditional or upbeat and modern

Above: the shock of the new enlivens Temple Bar

Left: the city boasts over 800 pubs, many with elaborate old frontages and appealing decorative features

Temple Bar

Many visitors to Dublin today are lured by the action in the very recently developed Temple Bar area, on the south side of the Liffey. The internationally famous Irish rock band U2 had a notable influence on the development here when their consortium purchased the art deco Clarence Hotel; the Kitchen is still one of the most exclusive nightspots in town. Along with the flourishing of bars and trendy clubs has come an increase in up-market boutiques, bistros and galleries, making this once run-down area lively, colourful and fun to explore. It's a gathering place for Dublin youth.

In the early '90s Temple Bar was in danger of sinking under the weight of its own success, beneath a tide of stag parties and drunken weekenders drawn here from across Europe. Balance was restored, however, with the introduction of a summer programme of free arts events, including street theatre and open air markets. This has ensured that there's something in Temple Bar for everybody, including the children. Indeed, the Ark has developed as a massive arts centre designed exclusively for work by, for and about children – perhaps not so surprising in a country where little ones are adored and tolerated almost everywhere.

The city is famous for its rock tradition, and in the bad old days before the Celtic Tiger economy and the cyber-revolution, music was one of the last outlets for youngsters hoping to escape unemployment and poverty. The Sound Training Centre in Temple Bar gives many children the chance to work at one of the city's big recording studios, as well as training for lighting, stage, film and television production, helping to ensure a lively future for the city's youth.

Setting the world to rights with a Guinness and a smoke

Kilmainham Gaol

Below: the grille of an iron cell door; 14 ringleaders were executed here after the Easter Rising of 1916

The Easter Rising of 1916 was a curious event, tiny in comparison with the rebellion of 1798, for instance, with only about 2,000 people actively taking part in it. It was disastrously badly organised and commanded very little public support, but its martyred heroes glow in the imaginations of republican Ireland as icons in the struggle against British rule.

On Easter Monday, 24 April 1916, Padraic Pearse, at the head of 150 men armed with ancient rifles and farm tools, took over the General Post Office, where he solemnly read out a stirring document proclaiming the new Irish Republic. Meanwhile, volunteers took over other buildings – a brewery, lunatic asylum, factory and bakery. Many Dubliners were as bemused as the British forces by the collapse of the city into chaos, and, instead of joining the rebels, made tea for the British. The fighting lasted for six days, and on the Saturday Pearse surrendered. Over 400 people had died, much of central Dublin lay in ruins, and the leaders of the Rising were even less popular than they had been at the start.

The tide turned when the authorities had 14 of them shot in the yard at Kilmainham Gaol, including Pearse and James Connolly. From then on, they were republican heroes. The release of hundreds of Irish internees later that year (among them Arthur Griffith, founder of Sinn Fein, Éamon de Valera and Michael Collins) did nothing to assuage the bitterness that surrounded the aftermath of the Easter Rising.

Today Kilmainham Gaol, last used as such in 1924, is an excellent if grim museum documenting the Irish struggle for independence.

Far left: the chilling cell block at Kilmainham, where prisoners from the uprisings were held

Left: a contemporary view of a prison visit sets the scene in stark black and white

THE EAST

The counties immediately around Dublin constitute the Pale, the area most strongly influenced by English rule from Norman times onwards. What lay beyond the Pale was less easily subjugated and often perceived (accurately) as a threat to English interests. The pull of the capital ensures these eastern counties still receive a steady flow of visitors, though scenically (with the exception of Wicklow) they are not Ireland's most exciting regions. There are, though, a good many reasons to spend time here. They are enormously rich in history, layer upon layer of it, from prehistoric to recent times. The famous passage graves at Newgrange are Ireland's best-known neolithic site. Then there are Celtic High Crosses, the evocative monastic settlement of Glendalough, many later abbeys and churches, castles and several of Ireland's grandest houses and gardens. Horse-lovers will want to visit the Curragh at Kildare and the nearby National Stud. For walkers, the heather moors and wooded glens of the Wicklow Mountains bristle with opportunities. The best beaches in this region are in County Wicklow.

Spiral carvings on a massive boulder, their purpose unknown, mark the low entrance to the passage grave at Newgrange

Cooley Peninsula

North of Dundalk, a few minutes' drive takes you into the lovely scenery of the hilly, granite Cooley peninsula, attractive in its own right, but also overlooking tempting views of the Mountains of Mourne across the lough which divides the Republic from Northern Ireland.

Cooley is associated with one of Ireland's best-known myths, the Cattle Raid of Cooley, in which Queen Maeve, jealous of her husband's prize white bull, attempts to take it by force. Cuchulainn, a boy warrior, defeats her army and becomes the hero of the hour, but is mortally wounded during the battle.

Curiosities on the Cooley peninsula include the giant Proleek Dolmen, accessible via a footpath from the Ballymascanlon House Hotel, and the Windy Gap, a mountain pass closely hemmed in by cliffs and crags, and scene of an incident in the Cattle Raid epic.

The vast, weighty cap-stone of Proleek Dolmen, an exposed tomb from around 3000 BC, seems to balance precariously

Carlingford

One of the most enjoyable places on the Cooley peninsula is Carlingford, between the green slopes of Slieve Foye and the blue waters of the lough, with the Mourne Mountains beyond. This delightful village makes a great base for exploring the area, with several excellent pubs and guest-houses.

For its modest size, it has some imposing monuments, indicating that it was a place of some significance during the Middle Ages. King John's Castle stands on the north side of the harbour, a massive D-shaped fortress dating from the 13th century. Its opposite number is Greencastle, on the Northern Irish side of the lough. In the village itself are Taafe's Castle and the Mint, both fortified houses, and the old town hall, or Tholsel, an arched gateway.

Carlingford sprawls comfortably around its old harbour

Newgrange

The structure at Newgrange is believed to predate the mighty pyramids of Egypt by several hundred years

Newgrange is one of Ireland's most important archaeological sites, and is perhaps the most spectacular passage-grave in Western Europe. Dating from c. 3000 BC, it is possibly 1,000 years older than Stonehenge. The grassy tumulus stands in a sloping field above the road, overlooking the glittering snake of the Boyne and a vast sweep of quiet farmland. It is easily spotted because the front retaining walls are faced with brilliant white stones of quartzite. The nearest source for these stones is the Wicklow Mountains, south of Dublin, so thousands of tons of material must have been dragged huge distances. The tomb takes the form of a long passage covered by a vast mound some 100m across, and over 10m high at its central point. At the front is a low entrance formed by slabs of rock, and above it another rectangular opening, the roof-box. This sophisticated device is constructed with a narrow slit in the stone so that, once a year on the morning of the winter solstice, the rays of the sun illumine the interior of the tomb.

A guided tour takes you into the inner stone chamber of the tomb, from which three recesses lead. The magnificent dovetailed structure of the vaulted roof still keeps the water out. Other mysterious patterns are carved on the inner stones, some invisible from outside and presumably for some cult purpose. Stone basins contained the bones of the cremated dead with offerings of beads and pins.

Newgrange is by no means the only local antiquity. The nearby mounds of Dowth and Knowth also contain passage

tombs. As you look from Newgrange, over the lush pastureland enclosed by this sheltered bend of the Boyne, the shapes of numerous strange humps and tumuli are visible. There are other burial sites, about 40 in all, some of which have not yet been explored.

The Irish name for this giant graveyard is Brugh na Boinne, the palace of the Boyne. Its builders were a farming community who were apparently fairly settled and peaceful, clearing forests and raising stock. The looping River Boyne furnished them with a useful artery of communication and a natural defence barrier.

Egg-shaped grey stones are studded at intervals among the white quartz of the facing

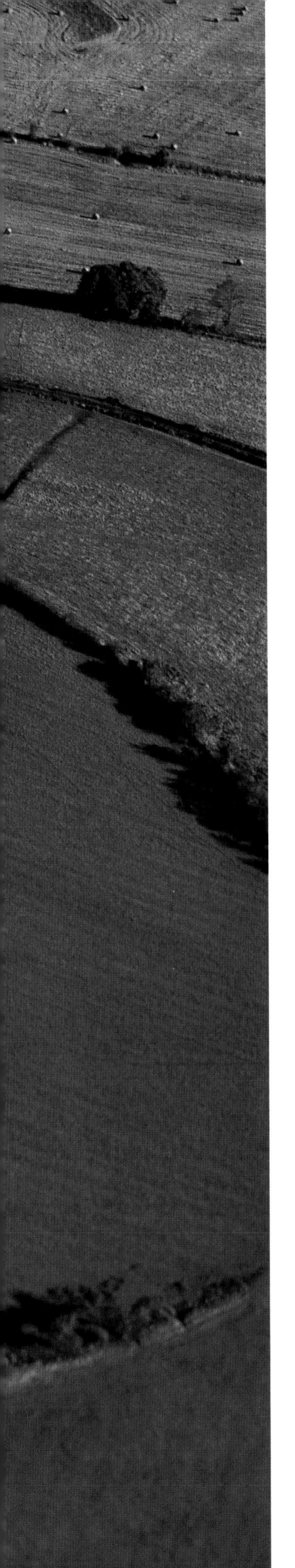

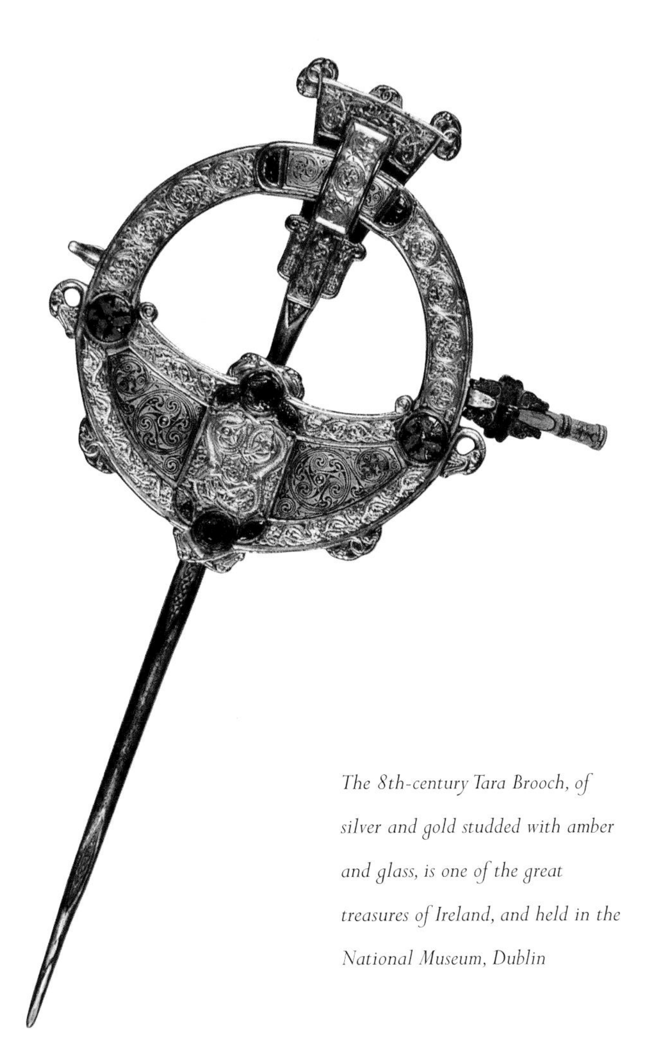

The 8th-century Tara Brooch, of silver and gold studded with amber and glass, is one of the great treasures of Ireland, and held in the National Museum, Dublin

Hill of Tara

Thirteen kilometres south of Navan is one of Ireland's most famous antiquities, the Hill of Tara. This shows evidence of occupation from many different periods, and was the symbolic seat of the High Kings until the 11th century. Its history is steeped in legends, but archaeological evidence suggests that some grim events must have taken place here. Various ring forts can be seen, though some were damaged in recent years by a group known as the British Israelites searching for the Ark of the Covenant. The site has probably always been associated with religious cults of some kind, though its influence waned after the arrival of Christianity. It was from this hill that King Laoghaire and the Druids first noticed St Patrick's defiant fire on the nearby Hill of Slane.

The Hill of Tara is now just a grassy flat-topped hill grazed by sheep, reached by a field path from the parking place. It rises only 100m or so from the surrounding land, but the views over the plains are very extensive. Various inconclusive mounds and earthworks indicate the locations of the old palaces, banquet hall and Bronze Age burial sites, and many artefacts have been unearthed. A visitor centre in a nearby church explains the site.

Tara's most significant event in recent times was a mass meeting called by the nationalist leader Daniel O'Connell which is said to have attracted over a million people. This alarmed the British Government, who suppressed O'Connell's activities and thus put one more nail in the coffin of a peaceful Anglo-Irish settlement.

An aerial view of the famous hilltop clearly shows the whole site, which includes a ring fort, a burial mound and the little bump, top left, of a Stone-Age passage grave

The little church is now the Tara Visitor Centre

Powerscourt

The pretty village of Enniskerry and the theatrical backdrop of the Wicklow Mountains add greatly to the appeal of this great estate, which covers about 5,500ha. Even the entrance drive is impressive – over a kilometre long.

James I granted the land to the 1st Viscount Powerscourt, Sir Richard Wingfield, in 1609. A magnificent house was designed by Richard Castle, whose Palladian handiwork can be seen all over Ireland. Unfortunately the great edifice burned to a shell in a disastrous accident in 1974, just after a long programme of restoration. Plans are afoot to recreate the house, but the phenomenal cost of the exercise has so far daunted enthusiasts. All that can be seen now are the splendid gardens, laid out on the south-facing slopes in front of the house which overlook the Great Sugar Loaf Mountain. They were first created in the mid-18th century soon after the completion of the house, but redesigned in the 19th century by the redoubtable Daniel Robertson with classical parterres and Italianate statuary. They contain glorious lakes with spouting fountains and winged horses, and magnificent specimen trees which grow to a prodigious height in this mild climate. Unusual touches include a Japanese garden (1908) on reclaimed bogland sporting little scarlet bridges, a pet cemetery dedicated to many faithful friends (Jack, Sting and Taffy), mosaic terraces made of beach pebbles from Bray, and neat, homely kitchen gardens. A garden centre, pleasant tea-room and a gift shop maximise tourist revenue.

An additional attraction about 6km away is the Powerscourt Waterfall, which plunges about 120m in a mare's-tail plume down a jagged rock face. There are excellent local walks around the valley below.

The sweeping ornamental gardens fully incorporate the mountain landscape beyond

A detail from a fine 19th-century wrought-iron gate in the parkland

The original mansion, burnt out in 1974, is now a magnificent shell

The National Stud

If you are at all interested in horses, one place you will certainly want to see is the Irish National Stud, based at Tully just outside the town. The valuable animals enjoy a standard of living many humans would envy, and their occupation may appeal, too. The stallions stay hard at work from January to July; the rest of the year is their 'holiday'.

The stud was set up in 1902 by the British, and transferred to the Irish state in 1943. Its eccentric founder was Colonel William Hall Walker, who believed that the stars influenced the horses' form. The stallion boxes are built with lantern roofs to allow heavenly bodies their full effect on the horses. Every time a mare foaled, Colonel Walker would cast its horoscope, and race or sell the progeny accordingly. The system, it is said, was uncannily successful.

Spring and early summer are the most interesting times to visit, when you will see new foals with the mares. Later in the year the Sun Chariot Yard holds promising yearlings whose paces are just about to be tested. Veterinary research is carried out at the stud, along with all aspects of the complex and rarified science of horse-breeding. The animals are not pets and should not be approached; apart from their extreme value, they can be fierce and may bite or kick.

The ornamental lake near the stable units has mineral-rich drinking water for the horses, said to encourage good bone structure. Also in the grounds are the ruins of the Black Abbey, dating from the 12th century, and the Irish National Stud Horse Museum, dedicated to all aspects of the equine species. The skeleton of the legendary steeplechaser Arkle is on display, as well as Pat Taafe's whip and the Duchess of Westminster's racing colours.

The Japanese Gardens, next to the Stud, offer a completely different attraction and are widely admired throughout Europe as the best of their kind.

Features in the gardens depict symbolically man's progress from birth to eternity

The National Stud gardens were created by Japanese gardener Eida and his son between 1906 and 1910

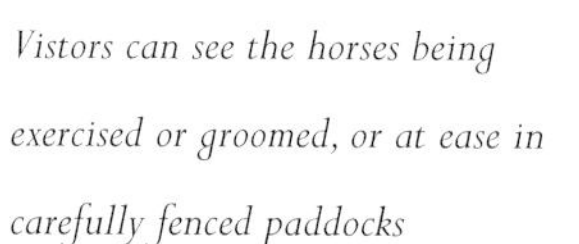

Vistors can see the horses being exercised or groomed, or at ease in carefully fenced paddocks

The Marriage Bridge marks a key point in the journey of life

The Curragh

The English and the Irish probably come closer to understanding each other through their mutual love of horses than in any other way. Ireland is currently estimated to have about 55,000 horses, including 15,000 racehorses.

Ireland is the heart of the bloodstock industry, where many of the world's best thoroughbreds are reared and trained. It also has facilities for every type of equestrian sport: flat-racing, steeple-chasing, show-jumping, eventing, hunting and trekking. Equestrian centres abound, and hunting is alive and well, with packs from Connemara's Galway Blazers to the Fingal Harriers of Dublin.

Horse-racing is more than a mere sport in Ireland; it is a passion, consuming and generating vast sums of money. The on-course betting turnover amounts to about IR£90 million a year, and thousands are avid students of form. The bloodstock industry turns over staggering amounts, aided by favourable government tax-breaks. Racing, however, was known in Ireland many centuries ago. The legendary Red Branch knights of Ulster raced, as did later Gaelic warriors, though it was then mainly a sport of kings. The Normans and Elizabethans loved it; Cromwell, with his characteristic lack of *joie de vivre*, tried to ban it as the work of the devil. During the 18th century racing was all the rage, and two neighbours in County Cork coined a new phrase with their epic cross-country dash between the spires of Buttevant and Doneraile churches – 'steeple-chasing'.

Racing accoutrements bring colour to the stables

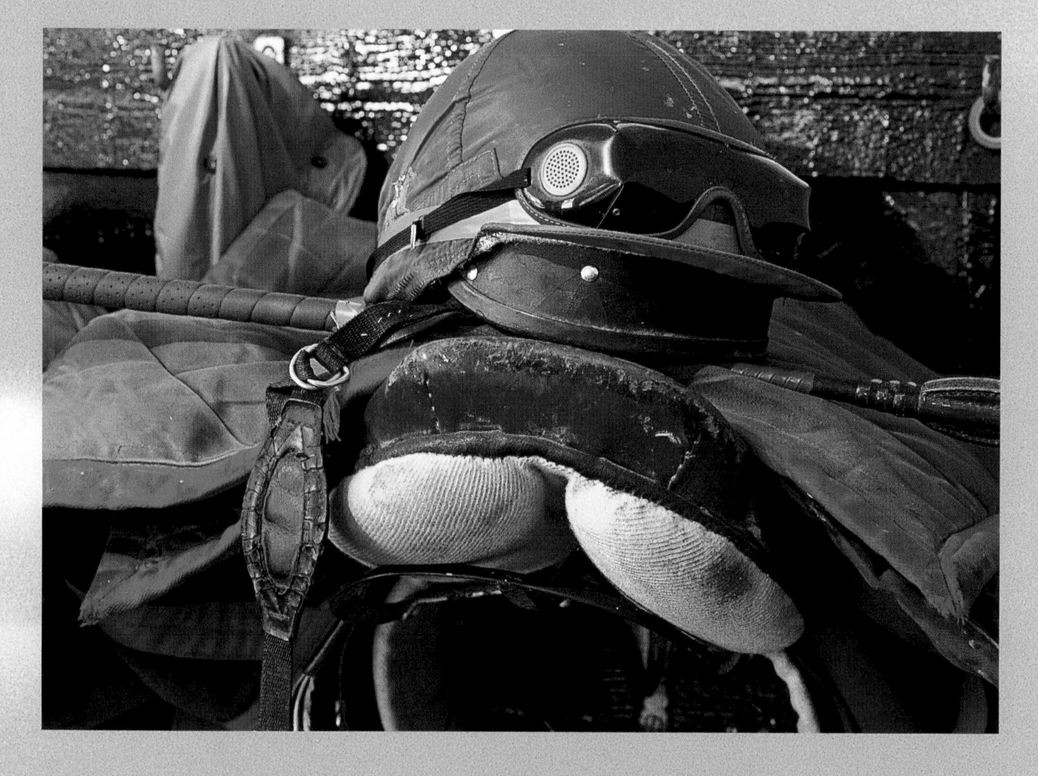

The Thrill of Steeple-chasing

Today, racing 'over the sticks' still has a great following in Ireland, although not nearly as much money is involved as in flat-racing.

The jumpers are usually gelded, which means that when their sporting days are over they cannot retire gracefully to sire lucrative strings of winning progeny, as the flat-racers do. None the less, the courage and stamina needed of both horse and rider in steeple-chasing make it an exciting and highly respected sport.

Jockeys, trainers and owners gather in the winners enclosure

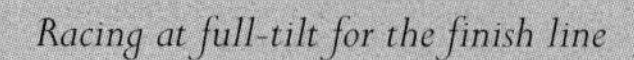

Racing at full-tilt for the finish line

Glendalough

This collection of monastic remains is one of the most important in Ireland. Coach parties visit it from Dublin, and the crowds have brought about a tawdry rash of souvenir shops, pubs and cafés in the local villages. Once away from this, however, the utter peace and beauty of the location are captivating, perhaps more than the ruins themselves.

It is easy to see why St Kevin sought solitude here in the 6th century, but his plans were somewhat thwarted. Beset by acolytes and lovelorn women (whom he treated brusquely by thrusting into nettles or pushing in the lake), he eventually set up a large religious settlement here, which held great sway until it was attacked by Vikings in later centuries and was at last overrun by English forces in 1398, after which its influence declined.

The ruins stand around two lakes in a beautiful wooded valley sheltered by great spurs of the Wicklow Mountains. The main concentration can be seen near the Lower Lake, by the visitor centre, where traffic converges. This modern building contains an exhibition of religious antiquities and an audio-visual presentation of monastic life in Ireland – giving an intriguing overview of this aspect of Celtic history. From here you can take a guided tour or make your own way round the remains. The famous sites are the well preserved 30m Round Tower and the intact church often called St Kevin's Kitchen because of its chimney-like bell tower. Against the backdrop of the wooded slopes, this assembly of quaint stone rooflines and pencil spires is unforgettable. Also visible are the shells of the roofless cathedral and the Priests' House, and many crosses and gravestones.

Further up the valley (a pleasant walk or short drive) near the more spectacular and peaceful Upper Lake are various minor sights – a beehive cell, an early fort and another ruined church. St Kevin's Bed is a suitably masochistic rocky ledge high on a cliff-face (safely accessible only by boat) where the saint used to sleep. Keen walkers have an excellent choice of routes in this area – a national park information point is open in summer.

Early morning mist hovers magically in the valley

A venerable round tower creates a romantic viewpoint in this peaceful valley

Wicklow Mountains

These wild hills on Dublin's doorstep are a great boon to city dwellers. From the southern suburbs you can gaze at them on clear days; by public transport or car they take just half an hour to reach. If you have time enough you can even walk there on the 132km Wicklow Way, starting just outside Dublin in Marlay Park.

The rounded hills of ice-eroded schist and granite enfold a strange mixture of bleak, awesome glens and boggy plateaux, interspersed with welcoming Shangri-La valleys like Glendalough or the Vale of Avoca. The improbable cones of the Great and Little Sugar Loaf Mountains protrude suddenly from the surrounding contours, their granite caps more resilient than the rest. The wildness and emptiness of the mountains made them good hiding places after the 1798 rebellion, and during those troubled times they were full of insurgents fleeing the English soldiers.

Avondale

Deep in one of County Wicklow's most beautifully wooded areas is the birthplace and home of the 19th-century politician Charles Stewart Parnell, now a museum dedicated to his memory.

Parnell was one of Ireland's greatest campaigners for democracy and land reform. Though at first regarded as a dangerous revolutionary because of his association

Below: these rolling hillsides provide a handy escape for Dublin city-dwellers and walkers

Sheep have the high tops to themselves in the mountains near Lough Dan

with the Irish Land League, he eventually won Gladstone's abiding respect and persuaded many people that Home Rule was a viable option for Ireland. His career foundered abruptly after his long-standing liaison with the wife of a fellow Member of Parliament became public knowledge. Soon after divorce proceedings were instituted, Parnell was ousted from his political position and died of mental strain and ill-health.

The house is most interestingly furnished and contains many touching mementoes and political cartoons. Some of his eloquent love letters to Kitty O'Shea are framed on the walls, as is the extensive Parnell family tree, many of whose members died tragically . The grounds were taken over by the state in 1904 as a forestry school.

Avondale House, dedicated to the great campaigner for Irish independence

THE SOUTHEAST

In contrast to the wildness of western Ireland, the Southeast is mostly low-lying and docile. Rich pastureland watered by brimming rivers extends gently to a quiet coastline of long sandy beaches, estuarine mudflats of wading birds and low cliffs fringing deep bays. Ireland's most fertile farmland lies in the Golden Vale, making Tipperary one of the most prosperous inland counties.

The Vikings held sway over this region for many years, finding those broad estuaries and inviting harbours easy landings from which to torment the native Celts with pillage and nose taxes ('Pay up or we'll cut your nose off'!). Following their example, Strongbow invaded Ireland for the Anglo-Normans via Waterford in 1169, ostensibly to help Dermot MacMurrough regain his Leinster throne. In return, Strongbow received the hand of Dermot's daughter, the first dynastic alliance between Irish and Norman. But the Normans stayed on and their power grew.

The Gaelic MacMurrough Kavanaghs resented this and remained a thorn in the English side, rebelling every so often with unexpected ferocity. Cromwell finally broke their resistance, and is unaffectionately remembered here for his slaughter of hundreds of unarmed citizens at Wexford.

A delicate interlacing of stone at the Rock of Cashel

Bunting decks the pleasingly old-fashioned pub fronts of Parliament Street

Kilkenny

One of Ireland's most delightful towns, Kilkenny stands on a bend in the River Nore. It is packed with history (in summer, with tourist traffic too), and aspects of its medieval history are particularly well preserved. Discerning visitors are duly catered for with high-quality craft studios and good restaurants.

The most striking building is the castle, a stronghold of the prominent Butler family until the 20th century. Originally a Norman fortress, it gradually became more domesticated through the centuries. It saw conflict again, however, when anti-Treatyites occupied it briefly during the Civil War in 1922. After a massive restoration programme, the castle is once again on show. The well-proportioned 18th-century buildings opposite the castle have now been converted into an imaginative enterprise called the Kilkenny

The hammer-beamed picture gallery, lined with portraits and elaborate ceiling decorations, is the most memorable room of the castle

The rambling Tudor mansion of Rothe House, built around a courtyard, is now the local museum

Design Centre, where local artists produce high-quality crafts. A large retail outlet fronting the street supplies some of the best goods on sale in Ireland.

Kilkenny's historical importance formerly rivalled Dublin's, and several significant political events took place here. Interesting buildings are scattered through the old town, including St Canice's Cathedral, one of the finest 13th-century buildings in Ireland (although Oliver Cromwell used it to stable his horses in 1650).

The monuments of the black limestone known as Kilkenny marble are particularly impressive – one female statue wears a traditional Irish cloak. Next to the cathedral are a round rower, which can be climbed for splendid town views, and St Canice's Library, containing a valuable collection of rare early volumes. Other medieval churches include the Black Abbey, the ruined St John's Priory and St Francis's Abbey. The Tholsel (town hall) and the court-house date from the 18th century.

Wexford

For all its bloody history, the bustling small town of Wexford has a peaceful air. If you catch it during October when the acclaimed opera festival is in full swing, you will be left in no doubt that the town rates itself pretty highly, and rightly so.

The Viking name *Waesfjord* (harbour of the mudflats) is apposite. The River Slaney and several tributaries empty their silt-laden waters into the sea here, and Wexford's practicality as a deep-water port has long since been overtaken by its rival, Waterford. North and south of the town, large areas of mud on either side of the estuary provide a habitat for many thousands of wading birds. The 'Slobs', as the mudflats are known locally, are reclaimed land, and home to the Wexford Wildfowl Reserve.

The town itself straggles along the waterfront, several blocks deep. The bronze statue outside the tourist office commemorates Commodore John Barry, the brilliant naval officer who avenged his Irish ancestors by emigrating to Philadelphia and trouncing the English during the American War of Independence. The old centre is a cheerful mix of agreeable pubs, old-fashioned shops and plenty of decent down-to-earth eating places. The main historic monuments are the Westgate, dating from 1300, and the remains of Selskar Abbey, where the Anglo-Irish treaty was signed after the Norman invasion, and where Henry II spent many Lenten hours atoning for the murder of Thomas à Becket.

In the Bull Ring, Cromwellian troops slaughtered 300 hapless citizens as they prayed for mercy. Many others were put to the sword in one of the most appalling massacres of the Ironside invasion. When Ireland rebelled again in 1798, Wexford's inhabitants were among the most vigorous pike-wielders, as the statue in the Bull Ring indicates.

Just where the River Slaney broadens into tidal mudflats west of town, a popular attraction draws the crowds. The Irish National Heritage Park at Ferrycarrig recreates life in Ireland through about 9,000 years of history, up to Anglo-Norman times. Full-scale models of lake settlements, ring-forts, burial places and a Norman motte-and-bailey castle lie hidden among hazel groves and reed-beds in a large park.

Opposite: a reconstructed crannog, or lake dwelling, at the Irish National Heritage Park

Some 40 per cent of the world's population of Greenland white-fronted geese make the Slobs their home for eight months of the year

Wexford's pleasing waterfront along the River Slaney

Jerpoint Abbey

The dark, battlemented tower of Jerpoint Abbey rises above a bend on the road south from Thomastown. This is one of the most atmospheric religious ruins in the country, revealing an intimate picture of monastic life.

The basic structure of Jerpoint is an excellent example of the austere architectural style promoted by the Cistercians, a rising force in Europe throughout the 12th century. In these times, manual labour was expected of monks and was to be carried out in silence. A mystic, Augustinian approach to contemplation also meant a reviling of intellectual theological debate, and a distaste for gold and other art works. Monks dressed in white, and early Cistercian abbeys had neither façade nor sculpted entrances, relying inside on the play of light to lift the spirit heavenwards.

By the end of the 12th century, however, the love of material pleasure and beauty was starting to re-assert itself, and Jerpoint is famed today for its abundance of delicate sculpture. Bishop O'Dulany of Ossory, who died in 1202, may have been one of the founders and the figures on his and other tombs are known as 'mourners'. Much of the interior decorative work is attributed to sculptor Rory O'Tunney, and dates from the first half of the 16th century. Figures in late-Gothic style are carved into the double columned arcades.

In 1540 the abbey was dissolved, and its lands presented to the earls of Ormonde. Local people are still buried in the cemetery here, in a touch of continuity with the past.

The massive square tower dominates these fascinating abbey ruins

Vivid, deep carvings of an angel and a king share the side of a medieval tomb

Waterford

Waterford is by far the largest town in the Southeast and one of the few prospering industrial centres in the Republic, with a grand history and plenty to explore. This is essentially a Viking city, with many reminders of this period of its history among the buildings lying immediately behind the waterfront. Reginald's Tower (now the Civic and Maritime Museum) was built in 1003 as part of the old city walls, and served subsequently as royal residence, fortress, mint, prison and air-raid shelter. One of Waterford's most interesting recent developments is the heritage centre housed in the disused church of St Peter's in Greyfriars Street, where the best finds from Waterford's Viking and medieval past (excavated during preparations for a new shopping centre) are excellently displayed.

A visit to the crystal factory, just outside the town centre, is a must for visitors. The history of Waterford glass started in the late 18th century, when George and William Penrose set up a factory here in 1783. It thrived for 68 years, before the disastrous economic conditions of 1851 caused its closure, and it would be another century before Waterford once again became a flourishing centre for glassworks. Free factory tours take place every weekday morning, and you can see each stage of manufacture. Basic ingredients of glass are silica and potash; lead crystal also requires a significant quantity of lead oxide in powder form. The lead gives the glass its particular qualities of brilliance and capacity to refract light, and also makes it very heavy. The ingredients are heated to 1,200°C over many hours, then hand-blown and skilfully shaped before cooling. Finally the glass is cut with deep grid-like patterns, the air filling with minute particles and the screech of carborundum and diamond wheels. You will see Waterford Crystal in grand houses throughout Ireland; today, a modern version of one of those glittering droplet chandeliers will knock you back several thousand Irish pounds.

Right: you can admire the work of the traditional glass blowers on the factory tour

Below: Reginald's Tower was named after the Danish governor who instigated it in AD 1003

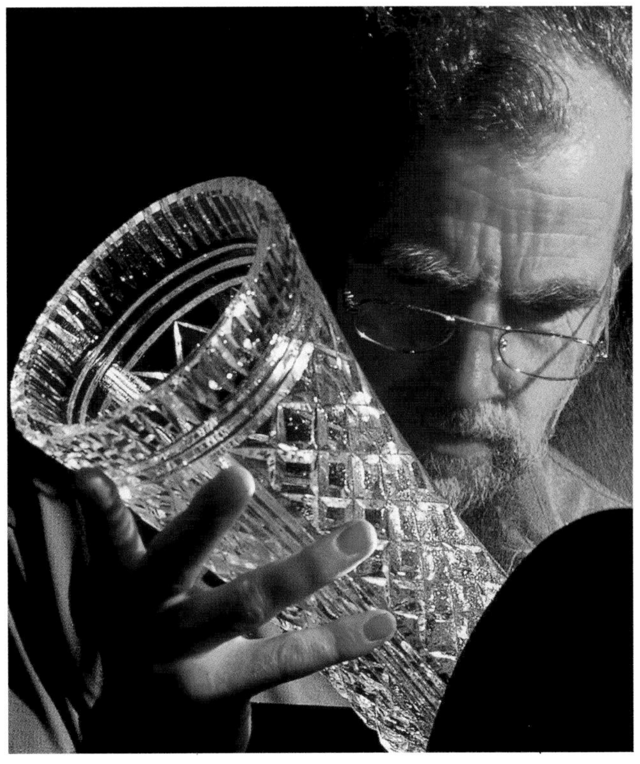

Waterford's most famous product is sought the world over for its luminous qualities and high craftsmanship

Below: a restaurant sign celebrates the town's Viking heritage

Clonmel

Clonmel is Tipperary's county town, a prosperous and pretty place with plenty of life and, if home-grown novelist Laurence Sterne's writings are anything to go by, some whimsically rum goings-on. Sterne lived during the 18th century and is best known for his picaresque novel, *Tristram Shandy*. Other writers have connections with the town: Anthony Trollope worked for a while in the local post office, and George Borrow, the 19th-century traveller, was at school here.

There are no outstanding sights in the town, but it has lots of pleasant shops and eating places, and stands on the edge of some extremely picturesque touring country. The circular drive to the south, along the Nire and Suir valleys, is very well worth taking on a fine day. So are trips into the unspoilt Comeragh Mountains near by.

The town was once an important stronghold of the powerful Butler family. Its Main Guard replaced the court-house destroyed in the Cromwellian siege. The West Gate dates from 1831 and stands on the site of an earlier medieval gateway. Near St Mary's Protestant church are sections of the old 14th-century walls which defended the town against Cromwell for longer than any other Irish town. A few churches have minor points of interest; several have eye-catching 19th-century, 'streaky bacon' coloured brickwork.

Clonmel is famed for its field sports, notably fox-hunting and hare-coursing. It is a great centre of the greyhound world, and the sleek animals can often be seen being exercised along the road, much as racehorses are in Kildare.

Discover a gently rolling landscape of pretty valleys and low, heather-clad hills around the town

Greyhound Spiral Nikita shows a champion's lines, bred for speed, at Newpark Stud

A view of the town through the narrow arch of the West Gate

Comeragh Mountains

Despite the high tech boom and the influx of factories and industry, most of Ireland remains agricultural with an emphasis on dairy farming. The area loosely referred to as the 'Golden Vale' stretches from the valleys of the River Suir and takes in Mitchelstown in County Cork, the valleys of the river Blackwater and parts of Limerick. Over them, however, the Galtee, Knockmealdown and Comeragh Mountains offer protection from the elements as well as romantic spots for hiking and pony trekking.

A bit off the tourist beat, this region offers a real peek into the heart of Ireland's cultural and economic heartlands, and is well worth the detour. Blessed with rich and fertile soil, it was in this area tenant farmers rose up against Anglo-Irish landlords, and the Land League movement of the 1880s fought some of its greatest battles. Pony trekking tours begin from the little village of Ballmacarbarry into the Comeragh Mountains whose peaks, at more than 750m, are the highest in County Waterford, extending southwards towards Dungarvon to become the Monavullagh Mountains.

A quiet road threads a valley in the beautiful Comeragh Mountains

A brilliant shaft of low autumn sunlight brings the landscape to verdant life

The Rock of Cashel

Stories tell how the devil bit a huge chunk out of the Slieve Bloom Mountains, then spat it out in disgust in the Golden Vale when he saw St Patrick preparing to build a great church. This erratic outcrop of limestone among the patchwork plains of rich cattle pasture looks almost freakish enough to justify such a tale. The Rock of Cashel is a mere 61m high, but approached from below, the craggy outline of towers and gables crowning the hilltop looks most ethereal, especially in certain conditions of light or weather. Close up, the romantic image fades a little under the pressure of tourism.

Cashel has long been a place of great significance, and rivalled Tara as a royal seat for the kings of Munster from the 4th century AD. St Patrick arrived in about AD 432 and converted King Aengus, who became Ireland's first Christian ruler. Among many legends associated with this event, St Patrick is alleged to have used a shamrock leaf to illustrate the nature of the Holy Trinity. During Aengus's baptism, the saint accidentally drove his crozier through the king's foot,

Above: a carving of a shamrock in the grey stone commemorates the influence of St Patrick

Remarkably well preserved is the 12th-century stone arch doorway

The craggy roofline of the buildings lends further grandeur to the Rock

but he did not complain and his wound was only discovered later. A shocked St Patrick asked why he had said nothing, and the king replied that he had assumed the suffering was some sort of initiation rite, emulating the pain of Christ.

The buildings now visible on Cashel date mainly from the 12th and 13th centuries. Earliest of these is probably the Round Tower, remarkably preserved, with an entrance doorway 3.5m above ground level. The Irish Romanesque Cormac's Chapel is ornately carved with beasts and human figures. A sarcophagus in the Chapel is said to be the tomb of Cormac, the bishop-king of Munster, who presided during Cashel's great time of influence in the 12th century. The roofless 13th-century cathedral, the largest building on the Rock, with tall lancet and quatrefoil windows and a later central tower on Gothic arches, witnessed a particularly unpleasant act of Cromwellian barbarism when Lord Inchiquin besieged the town in 1647. The citizens fled to sanctuary in the cathedral, whereupon turf was piled up around the walls and set ablaze, roasting hundreds to death. Attempts were made to repair the building, but it gradually declined and in 1749 Cashel's main place of worship was moved down to the town.

Cahir

The fortress in the centre of this small town on the Suir River is in fine condition after recent restoration work. Cahir Castle dates mainly from the 15th century with many later alterations, and was formerly a stronghold of the powerful Anglo-Norman Butler family, Dukes and Earls of Ormond. Queen Elizabeth I's favourite, the Earl of Essex, rammed a few cannon-balls into its masonry in 1599, but it went on to survive Cromwellian times little scathed. The huge walls enclose three separate 'wards', outer, middle and inner, the inner one guarded by a gate with a portcullis. Whitewashed rooms in the keep contain armour displays and period furnishings from the 16th and 17th centuries.

Cahir's fortunes waxed and waned through the centuries, but in peace time it developed an important milling industry introduced by local Quakers. The town is something of a time warp, and some of its shops and houses

The grim battlemented walls of Cahir's 15th-century castle have withstood several serious batterings

appear little changed for decades. Another agreeable feature of the town is its evident lack of religious or political bigotry: Protestants and Catholics used to worship simultaneously in its ruined church, separated only by a curtain wall.

The Swiss Cottage, lying just outside the town on the Clonmel road, is a local curiosity. This quaint thatched building with its eyebrow windows and corkscrew timbering

Gaily painted shopfronts by the bridge in Cahir

looks like something out of *Hansel and Gretel*, and was designed in 1810 by the Royal Architect, John Nash, for a scion of the Butler family.

Another attraction, in the nearby Mitchelstown, are the caves. Believed to be the largest system of river-formed limestone caverns in Ireland, where minerals in the rocks have caused spectacular colorations. Though privately owned, they remain pleasantly uncommercialised.

Stalactites and stalagmites become one in the spectacular Mitchelstown Caves

GUINNESS
IS GOOD
FOR YOU

ITS AN ILLUSION

THE SOUTHWEST

In any tourism league, Ireland's southwestern corner ranks high, and for many people the counties of Cork and Kerry represent the best that Ireland can offer for scenery, charming towns, mild climate and places of interest. The influence of the Gulf Stream keeps frost permanently at bay and, though Atlantic storms can be severe, sheltered regions lend themselves to superb subtropical gardens and a great range of flora and fauna. There is a huge variety of things to do and see, and events such as Kinsale's annual gourmet festival raise both standards of cuisine and the region's popularity with visitors. The high quality of local ingredients helps: seafood, good beef and rich dairy products now available everywhere belie the terrible sufferings of the Famine years.

Few would argue that the islet-strewn peninsulas trailing westwards to the Atlantic offer the best scenery, where the blue water of never-distant sea sets off the brilliant rain-washed emerald of fields and mountains. Here the pace of life is slow and gentle, and the ambience unmistakably Irish, perhaps most noticeably in the Dingle peninsula, one of the largest Gaeltacht (Irish-speaking) regions. Traditional Irish music can be heard all over the region, particularly in Dingle.

Dan Foley's, at Anascaul, is instantly recognisable

Bathers enjoy the shallow seas at the magnificent sand-bar of Inch Strand, famous as a main location for the film Ryan's Daughter

It is now difficult to imagine a community living year-round on the windswept Blasket Islands

Dingle Peninsula

A tour round this remote, Irish-speaking westerly extremity offers many things: superb coastal scenery with peaceful beaches and scattered islands; grand mountains and lush, fuchsia-splashed countryside; a rich assortment of antiquities; and a lively music scene and excellent seafood restaurants based on the charming fishing port of Dingle.

If archaeology does not thrill you, the scenery certainly will, especially when the wild Blasket Islands appear as you round the Slea Head promontory. The Blaskets are now occupied by a handful of summer visitors including the former Prime Minister, Charles Haughey, and there are plans to renovate some of the abandoned houses. The last native inhabitants moved to the mainland in 1953, the people no longer willing to confine their lives within this tiny community. The Blaskets have inspired a thriving

Small but perfectly formed – the distinctive Gallarus Oratory

literary tradition: Maurice O'Sullivan's *Twenty Years a'Growing* and Tomás Ó Crohan's *The Islandman* are two of the best-known accounts of island life. Summer boat trips visit the islands from Dunquin, where the film *Ryan's Daughter* was made. The Blasket Centre at Dunquin (Dun Chaoin in Irish) contains an exhibition on island life and literature.

Towards the ragged northwest of the peninsula are two interesting historic monuments. One is the Gallarus Oratory, a tiny but perfectly preserved church built of neatly packed unmortared stones. It dates from between AD 800 and AD 1200 and still keeps the rain out, though its roof-line is sagging slightly. A couple of kilometres up the road is Kilmalkedar, another early church from about the 12th century, roofless but bearing fine Romanesque carvings in purplish stone.

Touring the Peninsula

Starting points for the famous 'Ring of Kerry' drive are Castlemaine (north of Killorglin), or Tralee. For scenic drama a clockwise tour is recommended (although the scenery at first is quiet and undramatic) with good dune beaches at Inch and small hamlets like Anascaul, with its two unusual pubs; the strange, secretive tarn to the north, Anascaul Lake, is worth a brief detour.

Dingle is the peninsula's main tourist centre, constantly lively during the summer. It is by no means undiscovered, as anyone arriving during its festival season (July–August) will note, but it never seems quite as overcrowded or touristy as Killarney. The town is extremely well-kept, with restored shop-fronts and colourful inn-signs. The harbour is particularly appealing – bright fishing vessels moored in a lovely natural haven. In former centuries smuggling was a major source of income.

Beyond Dingle is Ventry, where you may see upturned *currachs* (canvas-covered canoes) on the beach. Follow the road marked Slea Head Drive round Ireland's most westerly point. The whole area is riddled with forts, souterrains, standing stones and crosses. On the hillsides you will pass a number of strange little stone huts known as beehives or clochans. There are over 400 in the area altogether, and the more perfect specimens may have been reconstructed from the original stones as storage places. Dunbeg, near Ventry, is one of the best sites: an Iron Age cliff-top fort with beehive huts near by.

By returning to Dingle again, you can start the final dramatic leg of this drive, over the Connor Pass, past the 953m summit of Mount Brandon. Once over the pass, Brandon Bay opens before you in a fantastic geological model of lakes, rivers and rock-strewn contours. The seafaring monk St Brendan set sail from these shores in the 5th century. In 1976, Tim Severin recreated this voyage in a similar craft of wood and leather to discover whether St Brendan could have reached America before Columbus (he concluded that it was indeed possible). Once down near sea level, the northern coastal strip is a quiet and easy drive past long beaches and more humdrum farmland.

Right: little boats in the harbour at Glasnabeg

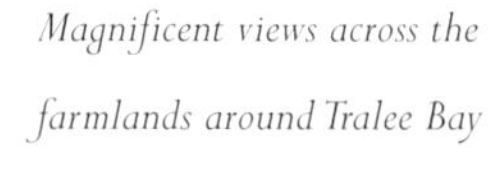

Magnificent views across the farmlands around Tralee Bay

Killarney

Every visitor to the Southwest has to see Killarney. The town itself may be given over to tourism and choc-a-bloc in summer, but the immediate surroundings of the Killarney National Park are not to be missed and, if you can evade the milling coach parties and wheedling 'jarvey-men' (pony-trap drivers), it takes on the grandeur of genuine wilderness. Macgillycuddy's Reeks, Ireland's highest mountains, lie just outside the National Park, but are clearly visible on fine days.

Out of the town, the choices for exploration are bewildering. To the south (the east shore of Lough Leane) lie the Muckross estate and various well-known beauty spots on the Kenmare road up to the pass called Moll's Gap. On the way, you may be diverted by the 15th-century Ross Castle by the lakeshore, and Muckross Abbey, a 15th-century ruin surprisingly well-preserved after a Cromwellian visit in 1652. The main pull, however, is Muckross House and the surrounding gardens and car-free parkland. To explore the extensive grounds, you can either accept a ride from one of the jarvey-men, or hire a bike. Muckross House is a furnished 19th-century neo-Tudor mansion designed by

Travelling in style, by jaunting car, by Lough Leane on the Muckross Estate

William Burn. Attached to it is a folk museum, where craftsmen demonstrate their trades, and several reconstructed farmhouses. The lakeside gardens have wonderful rhododendrons and azaleas, best in early summer. The Meeting of the Waters is a popular spot between the Upper Lake and Lough Leane, where arbutus trees flourish in the mild climate. Lake boats 'shoot the rapids' here, and close by is the Torc Waterfall, plunging 20m down a mountainside.

Beyond Muckross House the road winds on through woods, heather moors and mountains, becoming ever more beautiful, but requiring care at hairpin bends and tunnels.

Above: the comforts of pub-life in Killarney

Top: Pause at Ladies' View, for an unforgettable vista across the lakes of the National Park, towards the Gap of Dunloe

Killarney Viewpoints

Ladies' View is a place to pause for an unforgettable vista across the lakes of the National Park towards the Gap of Dunloe. The 'ladies' were Queen Victoria and her ladies-in-waiting, who presumably caught this view on a fine day and were duly impressed.

The Gap of Dunloe is Killarney's other great tourist attraction, a rugged glacial pass between the mountains, providing magnificent views of tarns and cliffs. It lies on the west side of the lake and is reached by heading north from the centre of Killarney. From Kate Kearney's Cottage, vehicular traffic is banned, so you must walk or hire a pony or jaunting car. Most of the tourists head no further than the spectacular Gap itself, but if you want more seclusion you can continue on foot through the lonely Black Valley, and down past Lord Brandon's Cottage (a handy tea-shop) to the lakeshore. There you can pick up a boat to carry you past the caves of Middle Lake, and over to the romantic ivy-clad tower of Ross Castle.

Ross Castle is a fine ruin dating from the 15th century; a tower-house and later dwelling house still remain, containing 16th–17th-century furnishings. Home of the local chieftains, the O'Donoghues, Ross Castle was the last place in Munster to fall to Cromwellian forces in 1652. The story goes that General Ludlow, hearing of a superstition that Ross Castle would never be taken by land, brought ships to sail up the lake, whereupon the defenders, hitherto defiant, immediately gave up their arms.

From Ross Castle, it is possible to take scenic boat tours of the lake, or to hire a rowing boat for a landing on Innisfallen Island. Here, against a landscape of gentle valleys and dark woods, are the ruins of Innisfallen Abbey dating from AD 600.

Page 64: mossy rocks and twisted old trees in the unspoiled Killarney National Park

A trip on Lough Leane will take you through wild, romantic countryside

Farming Country

One of the earliest surviving pieces of Irish literature, the *Tain Bo Cuailagne*, or Cattle Raid of Cooley, suggests that the Celtic obsession with land and animals has been an enduring way of life since neolithic times and will remain so.

The first unit of Irish currency was the cow, and a female slave sold for the value of six young heifers. When the Romans settled, the Irish scorned their delight in oysters, and a distaste for seafood in favour of decent, farmed livestock prevails amongst the older generation even today. Some of Ireland's finest cattle are raised in this part of the country.

For centuries the landscape was nurtured and cultivated by farmers who cleared the primeval oak woods and drained the peatbogs for pastureland, and small farming forms the not-so-distant roots of most Irish people, even today. Sheep, cattle, oats and barley have been raised since earliest times, while later crops such as flax and potatoes have waxed and waned according to the vagaries of economics.

However, membership of the European Union (EU) has resulted in Irish agriculture undergoing a rapid period of change and intensification, and government think-tanks are hard at work trying to preserve a way of life that it would be a tragedy to lose. One necessity is to counter migration to towns and cities, which has already severely depopulated rural Ireland– today 60 per cent of Irish people live in towns of 1,500 or more, and the country has a population density less than half the EU average.

Above: cattle grazing in the fields near Aghadoe

Left: a farmer with his herd of beef cattle

Bantry

Most people who tour south Cork pass through this fishing and market centre on the main coastal road. The town stands at the head of the long haven of Bantry Bay, sheltered by two of the hilly peninsulas that trail southwest from Cork's mainland. A statue of St Brendan gazes seawards from its square by the harbour. Bantry was twice an unsuccessful target for French invaders hoping to establish a base in a friendly Catholic enclave from which to overthrow the English. In 1689 a French fleet called in, offering support for James II, only to be rebuffed by William of Orange's supporters. In 1796 the revolutionary Wolfe Tone arrived with another French fleet, but was driven back by fierce storms. An alert local landowner, Richard White, sent urgent warnings to the English forces and was rewarded for his loyalty by a peerage.

His descendants still live in the splendid mansion of Bantry House, one of the most beautifully located houses in Ireland. The terraced Italianate gardens overlook a gorgeous sweep of Bantry Bay. The house amply repays a visit, its sumptuous rooms full of fascinating objects. In a renovated side courtyard is the Bantry 1796 French Armada Exhibition Centre. This lively museum recounts the history of Wolfe Tone's failed rebellion and displays articles recovered from the wreck of the frigate *La Surveillante*, which sank during the storms.

The little town stretches out around the horseshoe-shaped harbour

Wolfe Tone's Invasion

In 1796, Britain was once more saved from foreign invasion by the weather. On 16 December a French Armada of 43 ships set sail from Brest, bound for Ireland. From the start, it was a disaster, storms disrupting communications between the fleet. Soon the ships were separated and only 16 battered crews reached Bantry Bay with their commander, Wolfe Tone.

On Christmas Eve Tone was ready to make his attack, but fatally, he decided to wait for Hoche, the French commander. By the next day his chance of a landing had gone; savage gales had blown the ships out of the bay. Tone wrote in his journal, 'We were close enough to throw a biscuit ashore… The elements fight against us.'

Above: in an unrivalled position above the shoreline, Bantry House looks out over the bay

An aerial view clearly shows the sheltered harbour; Bantry House is at the centre of the photograph

Garinish Island and Ilnacullin Gardens

Ilnacullin, the Italian Gardens on Garinish Island, are reminiscent of a Maxfield Parrish fantasy, hardly what you'd expect in rural Cork, though the conical hills in the background may suggest a lesser Mount Olympus. However, such 'follies' or architectural fantasies are not uncommon in Ireland's traditionally bleak landscape, usually the creation of landed gentry who wished to create a more European feel against the background of the country's poverty and political problems, while helping to create work for the local populace.

Garinish Island was bought from the British War Office in 1910 by Annan Bryce, a Belfast-born MP, who enlisted the help of Harold Peto, a landscape designer famous for creating wild looking Mediterranean gardens which were the fashion at the turn of the last century.

Ilnacullin is considered his masterpiece, and against all odds – struggling with shallow soil and exposed, eroded rock – marvellous species of southern hemisphere and subtropical plants have been made to flourish, encouraged by the warm waters of the Gulf Stream which bathe the southern coast. The most unusual specimens include Australian fern trees, rare camellias from Japan, conifers from South America, scarlet berry climbers from China, *Cestrum newellii* from Mexico and the largest recorded specimen of *Dacrydium cupressinum*, or rimu tree, within Ireland or the United Kingdom.

The Martello Tower on the highest point of the island was the first of many, built to fend off a Napoleanic invasion expected in 1804–5. The remaining buildings, however, including the clock tower, a Grecian temple overlooking the sea, and flights of steps apparantly built for the private bathing of an Aegean princess, were additions by Peto and Bryce. Playwright George Bernard Shaw spent some time here working on *St Joan* in 1923, and Bryce gave the island back to Ireland as a gift in 1953.

The rocky shoreline at Garinish Point, Beara penisula

The layout of these extraordinary gardens was influenced by Harold Peto

Enjoy Italian style and architecture blended with an orderly jungle of flowering shrubs

A sweep of shingle beach at Sheep's Head – note the distinctive demarcation between rocky highland and habitable green foreshore

Mizen Head

Ireland's best loved modern poet, Seamus Heaney, was not the first to notice that the country's late night radio fog reports, melancholy in tone, were a poem in themselves, and Mizen Head, at the furthest outcrop between Dunmanus and Roaring Water Bay, figures prominently in an evening's somber litany of danger points.

Opened in 1910, the Mizen Head Signal Station has guided many a wary craft through black Atlantic storms and perilous fog and away from wave-tortured rock. In 1993 the station was made automatic, and the Keeper's House was turned into a visitor's centre the following year. It is now a local attraction, with meticulous upkeep of the engine room, and special exhibitions devoted to birds and sea or storm activity. Entrance is over a 58-m concrete suspension bridge, built in 1908, which spans a deep chasm in the rock. From the summit of the head at 241m, views to the south and west give a taste of the tension the keeper must have felt on a wild night. You can also see Three Castle Head, the ruins of the promontory fort of the O'Mahony chieftains.

On the north shore of Dunmanus Bay, Sheep's Head lies at the tip of the peninsula, commanding splendid views of the Caha Mountains on the north side of Bantry Bay.

The village of Ballydehob, at the base of the peninsula

Far right: scattered farmhouses in an idyllic setting above Dunmanus Bay

Kinsale

Kinsale has attractions out of proportion to its modest size and so is very popular. Its setting is seductive – tall slate-roofed houses sprinkled among the steeply wooded estuary slopes of the River Bandon. Its historic interest and fishing-village charm make it an appealing place both to stay (it has excellent accommodation) and to eat. From Kinsale you can easily explore both Cork City and the glorious coastal or inland scenery of south Cork. It is also a notable sailing and fishing centre.

During 1601–2, a Spanish force occupied Kinsale and were besieged by English troops. Irish allies of the Spaniards were routed, a significant step towards the establishment of the English order (and the decline of Gaelic power) in 17th-century Ireland. Soon afterwards the main players in this struggle, the O'Neill and O'Donnell clan chieftains, fled to Europe and abandoned their lands to English settlers. The town was spared a Cromwellian hammering, wisely backing the winning side. Later that century James II landed at Kinsale with French forces in an attempt to regain his throne, and from here he finally left Ireland, defeated.

Kinsale became an important English naval base, and Desmond Castle (now a heritage centre) held many French prisoners in Napoleonic times. The town is evidently proud of its history, which is well recorded in the local museum, a Dutch-style 17th-century town hall in the centre of town. Some of its most interesting exhibits relate to the sinking of the *Lusitania*. The court-room in which the inquest was held is a memorial to the 1,198 victims of the disaster.

Of Kinsale's two fortresses the most interesting is Charles Fort on the east side of the estuary, built in the late 17th century to guard the harbour entrance. One of the best-preserved examples of a star fort in Europe, it remained garrisoned until 1921. You can clamber over the ramparts and visit a military exhibition. The views of Kinsale from this headland are superb.

A ruined fortress stands on the lonely headland of the Old Head of Kinsale

Below: the town is famous for its colourful paintwork and floral adornment

Far right: brightly painted cottages add a splash of colour

Top, left and above: Kinsale is a gourmet's treasure trove of pubs and restaurants, celebrated in the annual festival of good food

Kinsale Gourmet Festival

During the first week in October, Kinsale is even more packed than usual, though its visitors may look more sleek and well-heeled than at other times of year. Kinsale's Gourmet Festival extends the normal tourist season nicely and is well publicised throughout Ireland, attracting a good many discerning palates from overseas, too.

This is a time for eating, when the town's excellent pubs and restaurants vie with each other to produce gastronomic delights. The emphasis is on local seafood, and the places to look out for are clearly advertised, displaying the Kinsale Good Food Circle sign.

A churning surf pounds the cliffs at the Old Head of Kinsale

Fishermen tend their nets at the harbour-side

Blarney

Everyone has heard of Blarney and, when coach parties clog the village, it seems as if everyone has come to see it, too. Tourists arrive for two reasons – to kiss that stone in Blarney Castle and to visit the large gift and craft centres that have sprung up near by. Quite why the Blarney Stone exercises such fascination is hard to fathom, but the superstition that kissing it endows you with Irish eloquence or 'blarney' is certainly appealing.

The stone is an oblong block of limestone located high among the battlements of a fine 15th-century tower-house, once a stronghold of the MacCarthys, former kings of Munster and Lords of Blarney. A Cormac MacCarthy supposedly strung Queen Elizabeth I along with honey-tongued promises and prevarications, until she exclaimed in exasperation, 'Blarney, Blarney! What he says he does not mean,' and thus the word entered the English language. To reach the stone, visitors must clamber up the tower steps (over 120 of them), join the inevitable queue (in high season, at least), and then lie down and lean backwards over a sheer drop. It looks awkward but is actually quite safe, even without the two strong-armed retainers there to grab your ankles. The stone is swabbed down regularly enough to prevent transmission of any nasty ailments. Some tout will offer to take your photograph while you are kissing the stone, but be warned, this is not a flattering angle!

The lush water gardens by the River Lee and the 19th-century Rock Close (a rock garden with fanciful wishing steps and druidical associations) make an attractive foil for the romantic ruin, and behind the castle is an elaborate Scottish baronial mansion called Blarney House, furnished in Victorian style.

In the village, craft and knitwear shops catch the purse strings, the most advertised being Blarney Woollen Mills, now a colossal hypermarket with a restaurant, hotel and coach-park attached. The smaller shops are rather more enjoyable, and there's a wide range of merchandise from all over Ireland on offer.

Kissing the Blarney Stone for the 'gift of the gab'

Far left: the tower floats above the trees in the morning mist

Left: a vertiginous view from the top of the battlements

Cork

Reflections on the waterfront

Cork takes pride in being the cultural and economic centre of the Southwest, and as the Republic's second city, constantly challenging Dublin's supremacy. It has always favoured ousting British rule, becoming known as 'rebel Cork' after supporting Perkin Warbeck (a Flemish impostor who in 1492 claimed to be Duke of York), and was a base for the Nationalist Fenian movement in the 19th century. Its prosperity was based on trade in hides, textiles, butter and wine. Industries such as ship-building and motor-manufacturing are no more, replaced by others such as the computer business. The centre's streets reveal Cork's mercantile past – tall, 18th-century bow-fronted houses and fine warehouses, steadily being restored.

The centre is built on reclaimed marshes ('Cork' comes from the Irish meaning 'marshy place') and the older part of the city is on an island embraced by two arms of the River Lee. The land rises steeply towards the heights of Shandon; several imposing church spires pierce the skyline. St Fin Barre's Cathedral was designed by William Burges in a flourish of white limestone steeples. Inside it is richly decorated – angels gazing down from a starry apse. On the Shandon side of town, St Anne's Church soars to a red and white pepper-pot tower surmounted by a golden weather-vane in the shape of a salmon. It houses the famous eight-bell carillon immortalised in the corny ballad known as 'The Bells of Shandon'.

On the island, Cork's commercial heart beats along the main thoroughfares of Grand Parade and St Patrick's Street. Old-fashioned department stores jostle trendy clothes

boutiques, but the newer and most chic shops are around the pedestrianised area near St Paul's Street. To the west lie elegant Georgian malls and the university. The Cork Public Museum – Republican history features prominently – is in the grounds of Fitzgerald Park by the Mardyke Walk, an attractive riverside breathing space.

Above: the old footbridge over the River Lee

Elegant old railings sag gracefully by the river

Limerick

Limerick is a significant city in terms of industry and population, vying with Galway for third place in the Republic. Energetic multi-million pound efforts to revitalise the centre are showing some success, particularly around its historic quaysides. Wharves and warehouses have been transformed into new business premises; its Norman and Georgian heritage is now carefully restored; and the town has come alive with attractive shops, restaurants and cafés.

This was originally a Viking settlement, by virtue of its strategic location at the mouth of the Shannon. The Normans expanded the town and built huge fortifications with curtain walls. In Cromwellian times the city was beseiged by English forces for over six months. Eventually, Limerick capitulated, and the infamous Treaty of Limerick was signed in 1691. Within two months the English reneged on their promises to grant the Catholic population religious and property rights, and instituted draconian measures against them. The Treaty Stone, on which the agreement was signed, became a potent symbol of all that was hateful about English rule. It can still be seen at the west end of Thomond Bridge, now sand-blasted clean in an attempt to erase the memories. Today Limerick is still a vehemently Catholic and Nationalist city.

Within the town centre the most notable monument is King John's Castle. First built in 1200, it still looks the part of a medieval fortress, though much restored. The tower is the oldest section, and houses an excellent and imaginative visitor centre. St Mary's Cathedral is the city's oldest religious building, dating mainly from the 15th century. Unexpectedly, it is a Protestant church. Its features include black oak choir stalls with carved misericords.

Replica thatched crannogs recreate neolithic times on the shores of Lough Gur

Below: the Norman fortress of King John's Castle stands out in the town

Lough Gur

Limerick's countryside is not especially noteworthy, but there is one little jewel tucked away in the southeast. Lough Gur is a beautiful crescent-shaped lake around which evidence of many early civilisations has been found. Antiquities include a wedge-tomb and a large stone circle at Grange. Cartloads of remains were discovered after the partial draining of the lake in the 19th century.

A display of ancient vessels helps to bring early history to life at the visitor centre on Lough Gur

FRUIT SWEETS
MINERALS
Rothmans
KING SIZE
Roses
Kellogg's
CORN
7UP
HAMLET
HB
ICE CREAM

THE WEST

Oliver Cromwell's famous declaration that Irish rebels could go 'to Hell or to Connaught' suggests he didn't think much of western Ireland. In times when soil fertility and accessibility were important considerations, these rain-swept, isolated outposts of barren limestone or waterlogged bog must have held few attractions. Famine struck this region particularly hard and emigration from Galway, Clare and Mayo has been high.

Until the 18th century, British influence was minimal, and the area is still firmly Gaelic in outlook, its population in tiny, scattered rural communities rather than towns and villages. The Irishness shows through, in speech, music, crafts, sport and attitude. Now, it is the West's very distinctiveness that many visitors find so appealing, and, above all, its scenery. These three counties encompass a rich variety of landscapes and sights, from the ghostly grey-white expanses of bare limestone in the Burren, and the wild coast and mountains of Connemara, where the Twelve Bens loom over flattering mirrors of water amid moorland and blanket bog, to the quieter Mayo, with lovely Achill Island.

Appreciate the slower pace of small-town life at Ballymoe, Co Galway

Achill Island

Mayo's western seaboard seems on the verge of disintegration, its straggling peninsulas anchored to the mainland by a thread.

Achill is the largest of these semi-islands, a rough triangle with sides about 24km long, linked to Curraun (itself a peninsula) by a modern road bridge over Achill Sound. Its quiet beaches and spectacular mountain scenery make it an appealing holiday destination; touring, by car or bike, surfing and angling are the main activities. In summer, boats make trips to coastal caves or in pursuit of the harmless basking sharks that haunt this coast. Keel is the main village, boasting shops, simple accommodation and a splendid sandy beach, with some dramatic formations known as the Cathedral Rocks at its furthest end.

The most scenic parts of the island can be seen from the Atlantic Drive (signed from the main road near the bridge), which leads past awesome cliffs, heather and gorse moors, and white cottages sprinkled against dark rocks. Beyond Keel, the road stretches towards Achill Head, rearing towards the Atlantic like a sea-monster.

Far left: the island is famous for its sandy beaches, and those at Keel and Keem have blue flag status

With little work available on the island, the scattered cottages are now often holiday homes

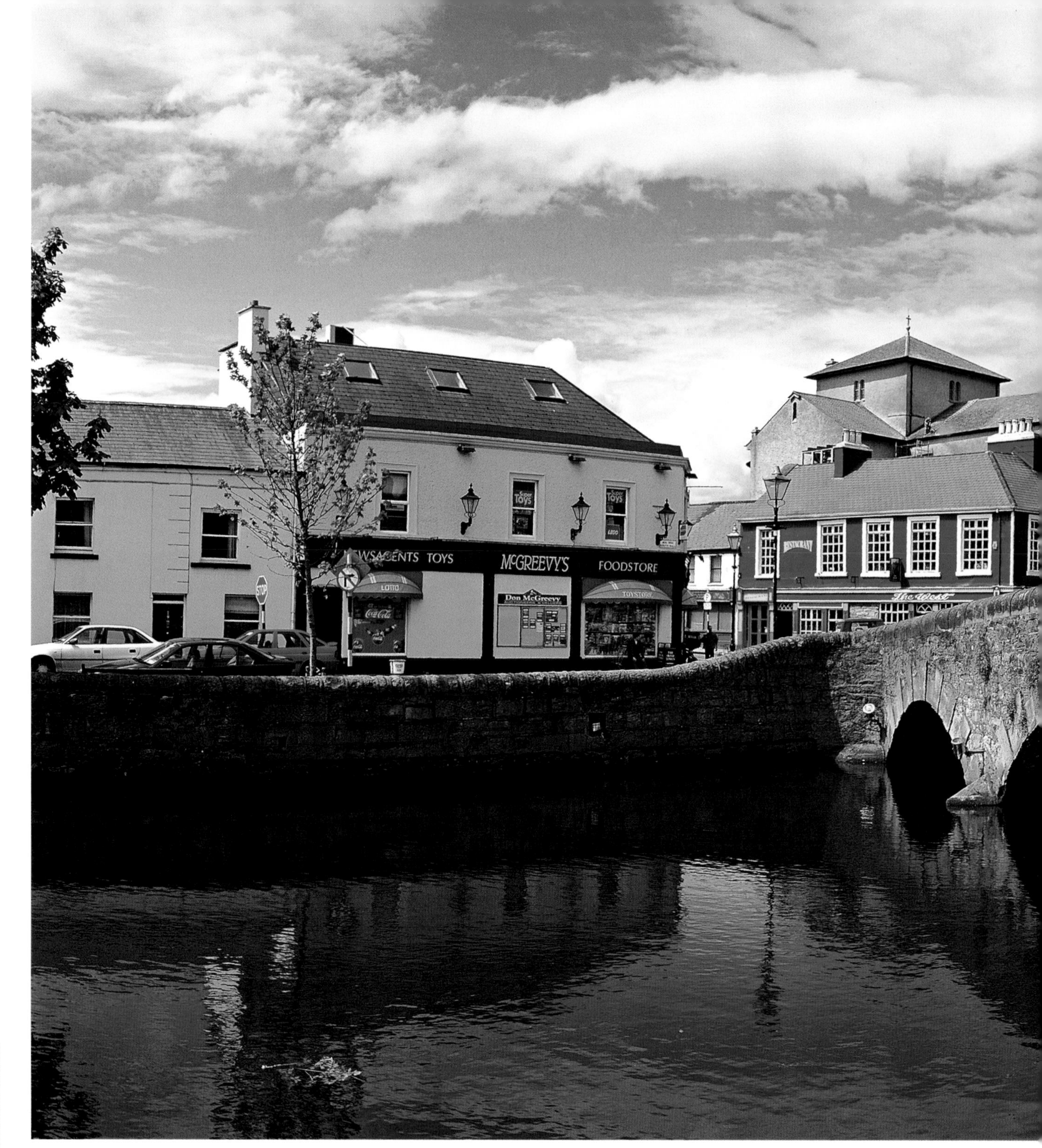

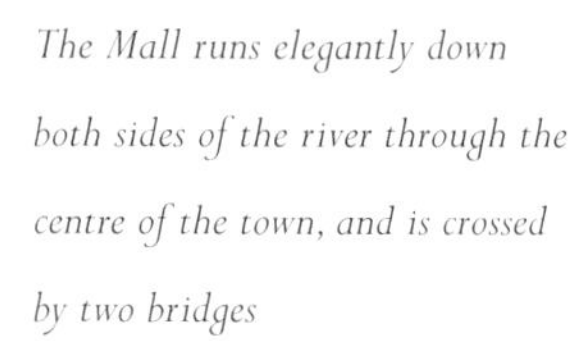

The Mall runs elegantly down both sides of the river through the centre of the town, and is crossed by two bridges

Below: a beached boat in Clew Bay

Westport

One of the most charming towns in Ireland's western region, Westport shows its Georgian origins clearly in its broad streets and canalised river flowing through a lime-fringed avenue called The Mall. It is set on an inlet of Clew Bay, where the Carrowbeg River flows into the sea. Many of its fine buildings remain, some carefully restored. The Protestant church is late Victorian (about 1880) and has charming art nouveau influences.

Westport was originally laid out as part of a great estate and, at the turn of the 18th century, prospered greatly from its textile industry. In 1801, however, local businesses collapsed as the Act of Union allowed a flood of cheaper products from England. By 1825, Westport's linen industry was virtually finished. Today, Westport is a market town and fishing centre, with a few good beaches near by.

Westport House stands in fine parkland about 3km outside the town, near Westport Quay. Designed by James Wyatt and Richard Castle, great architects of the 1730s, it is the seat of the Brownes, Marquesses of Sligo, and is County

Mayo's only stately home open to the public. Though highly commercialised in order to meet the colossal running costs, it is still a remarkable house, beautifully furnished inside with Irish Georgian and Victorian silver and antiques, Waterford crystal, Chinese wallpapers and a fine collection of paintings. The doors are Jamaican mahogany (the 1st Marquess spent time as a governor there, apparently one of its more benevolent rulers, who freed many slaves). The dungeons beneath the house date from an earlier dwelling, allegedly a castle belonging to the pirate queen, Grace O'Malley.

Pleasure boats on the lake at Westport House

The most ardent of the faithful will start their climb before dawn

A statue of St Patrick waits to bless pilgrims at the foot of the rocky path, with the unmistakable peak of the holy mountain behind

Croagh Patrick

The brooding, conical outline of this mountain dominates the skyline all around southwest Mayo. It is associated with St Patrick, the site of his Lenten fast and legendary 'Pied Piper' act with the snakes. Each year, on the last Sunday in July, pilgrims make an arduous ascent, some barefoot.

On clear days, the summit gives magnificent views over Clew Bay to the Partry Mountains and Connemara. If you are sensibly shod, you can climb Croagh Patrick in a couple of hours.

Knock

Knock's pedigree dates back over a century, when it was suddenly transformed from a humdrum little bog village into one of the most revered Marian shrines in Christendom. It is now the 'Lourdes of Ireland' with a vast new basilica, constantly thronged by pilgrims.

Its present high profile in the Catholic world is due in large part to the energies of a local priest, Monsignor James Horan. He battled with the authorities for an airport which, despite early descriptions as 'a foggy, boggy white elephant', has opened up the northwest region to tourist traffic since its eventual inauguration in 1986, seven years after Pope John Paul II made a celebrated visit to Knock. The commercialised religiosity of innumerable souvenir stalls may offend the purist, but today Knock attracts more pilgrims than ever, around one and a half million a year.

On a dark and stormy night in 1879 two village women saw, on the gable of the parish church, an apparition of the Virgin Mary, with St Joseph and St John. It lasted a couple of hours, then faded away gradually, and the sight was confirmed by 13 other villagers. Witnesses were cross-examined by a commission of enquiry, and some 50 years later, three surviving witnesses were again independently interviewed, and firmly maintained every detail of what they had seen, giving an unnerving veracity to their story.

The original church still exists, the gable where the vision was seen is now preserved behind a glazed oratory. It has fine features inside, notably stained glass by Harry Clarke (1889–1931). The new hexagonal church, designed to hold a congregation of many thousands, was completed in 1976. Its 32 ambulatory pillars each contain stone from a different Irish county, and the windows represent the four provinces: Connaught, Leinster, Munster and Ulster.

Left: a range of souvenirs for sale in the pilgrimage town of Knock

Below: pausing for breath on Croagh Patrick

Above: huddled cottages and a windswept tree on Inishmore

Right: an aerial view over Inishmore reveals a mere scraping of fertile green over the limestone surface of the island

Left: Dún Aengus fort perches on a precipitous cliff edge, exposed to the elements

Aran Islands

The cracked limestone terrain of the Aran Islands, lying about 45km out in Galway Bay, links them geologically with the Burren, in County Clare. The islands are flattish, but tilt towards massive sea cliffs in places. Making a living on these bleak rock platforms, virtually treeless and exposed to the full brunt of Atlantic storms, has always been a struggle. Large areas have no natural depth of soil and the islanders have painstakingly created fields from a mixture of sand and seaweed compost, protecting them with an intricate network of dry-stone walls.

Today's dwindling population of islanders subsist on their age-old livelihoods of fishing and farming, and increasingly on tourism. Many speak Gaelic and a few still wear traditional Aran dress. The high-prowed canvas fishing boats called *currachs* are used around here, and you may see them being carried up from the beach over the men's heads, like giant beetles, to protect the skin from the rocks.

Aran has always inspired a strong tradition of literature and oral story-telling; J M Synge set his play *Riders to the Sea* here, and the classic film, *Man of Aran*, made by the Irish-American director, Robert Flaherty, in 1934, depicted the harsh life on the islands.

Inishmore is the largest and most visited island. You can explore by bike, on foot, take a minibus or hire a pony-trap ride along its 12km spinal road. Inishmore has a wealth of ancient monuments, notably one of Ireland's outstanding prehistoric sites, the remarkable cliff fort of Dún Aengus. Three concentric horseshoe rings of stone perched atop mighty cliffs seem an odd place of refuge, so exposed to the elements and with a sheer drop to the roaring sea below. Its precise age and purpose are still a mystery.

The smaller islands of Inishmaan and Inisheer both have small fortresses, churches and folk museums to visit.

Simple, stylish furnishings in Yeats's tower retreat

Thoor Ballylee

In 1917, W B Yeats found this evocative 'ivy-covered tower', conveniently close to his friend and patron Lady Gregory, who lived at Coole Park. Thoor Ballylee was a fortified residence built by the Anglo-Norman de Burgo family during the 14th century.

Then in his 50s and newly married to his young bride George Hyde-Lees, Yeats purchased the derelict tower-house for £35 and spent intermittent periods of the next decade there with his new family, converting the interior into simple but stylish living and sleeping quarters. The 'winding stair' image which repeatedly appears in his poetry refers to the stone steps leading up the tower. From the battlemented roof-top, views extend over the placid meadows by the nearby millstream to the Slieve Aughty Mountains.

Many of Yeats's more mystical writings were produced here, notably *The Tower* and *The Winding Stair* (not generally his most admired work); by this stage his disillusion with the Irish political scene was taking effect and he sought relief in seclusion and mythology.

In 1928 Yeats abandoned the damp tower for warmer climes and died in France in 1939. The Kiltartan Society took over the decaying tower in 1961 and fully restored it in Yeatsian style, putting many documents, first editions and manuscripts on display.

An ancient bridge and a more ancient tower,
A farmhouse that is sheltered by its wall,
An acre of stony ground,
Where the symbolic rose can break in flower.

(*Meditations in Time of Civil War*)

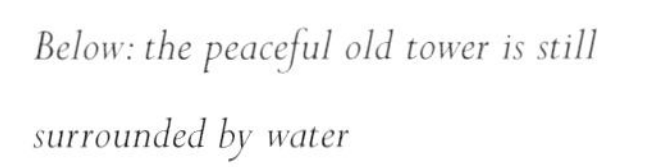
Below: the peaceful old tower is still surrounded by water

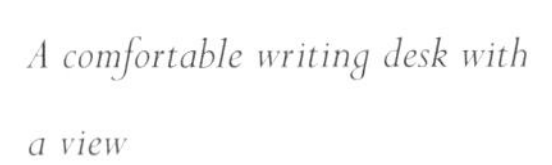
A comfortable writing desk with a view

Galway

Despite its size, Galway has an intimate, village-like atmosphere and seems a place where everyone knows everyone else. There is always plenty going on – a festival just about every month, an innovative theatre, concerts, lively pubs and restaurants. Besides its prestigious university, where students can take their degrees in Gaelic, Galway has several Irish language schools. It is perhaps Ireland's most enjoyable and upbeat city, full of vivacity and character and increasingly frequented by younger visitors in search of 'good *craich*' (fun). It hosts high-calibre Irish folk groups and its sporting prowess is a source of pride, particularly in games such as Gaelic football and hurling.

Galway's prosperity was founded on its strategic location at the lowest bridging point of the River Corrib. Founded by the Anglo-Normans in the 13th century, it became known as the City of the Tribes, a reference to the 14 leading families who held sway quarrelsomely in its early history. In its heyday, Galway was a significant European trading centre; its traditional vessels, the elegant lateen-rigged Galway hookers, traded food and fuel for livestock from the Aran Islands, or smuggled contraband from France and the Channel Isles.

By the western mouth of the river are the remains of a Gaelic-speaking fishing community known as The Claddagh. The cottages have now been replaced by tidier municipal housing, but old photographs and artefacts in the city's museum show how it looked.

Above: brightly restored shop-fronts in the narrow steets distinguish this flourishing and most bohemian of Irish cities

Below: where Galway Bay starts to open out, the Spanish Arch is a rare survivor of the old city walls

Left: the buskers of Galway are kept busy at Oyster Festival time

The Burren

From a distance parts of this treeless limestone plateau in north Clare look bleak, but a closer exploration reveals that the area is astonishingly rich in plant-life, playing host to over 1,100 of the 1,400 species found in Ireland. Although the stone surfaces have been scraped clean by the elements, every crack and hollow contains some fragile vegetation, absorbing moisture and nutrients from minimal resources. Alpine species flourish next to those from Mediterranean shores: rare saxifrages, gentians, maidenhair ferns and orchids. The best time to visit the Burren for flowers is undoubtedly in May or June.

Within a couple of hours you can drive across the Burren on the major road from Ennis to Ballyvaughan – and get an idea of the landscape of ancient domed hills and grey-white crazy paving. But this moonscape reveals its real charms only to the sharp-eyed observer on foot, so take a picnic, and leave your vehicle at some stage. A 30km waymarked trail, the Burren Way, runs from Ballyvaughan towards Doolin.

Hardy, low-growing alpines like this thrift grow in the cracks and fissures (grikes) of the natural limestone pavement

The southern section of the Burren is characterised by seasonal lakes called turloughs, which ebb and fill as the region's water table changes. Gradually, rainwater falling on this limestone plateau finds its way underground into a maze of caves and subterranean channels. Most are too dangerous for novice investigations, but one has been opened and is worth a visit; Aillwee Caves, south of Ballyvaughan is a commercial operation, but the cavern itself is left reasonably natural apart from pathways and illumination.

Parts of the Burren are actually quite fertile, supporting some farming and herds of feral goats. Other areas seem inhospitably bare, a shock after the lushness of most of Ireland. For centuries before the advent of tourism the sparse population of the Burren lived in grim poverty.

As you cross the central spine of the Burren look for ancient tombs, such as the 4,500-year-old Poulnabrone Dolmen, or the Gleninsheen wedge-tomb, easily spotted beside the R480 near Caherconnell.

A huge prehistoric dolmen looms out of the landscape like a piece of modern sculpture

Roundstone

Connemara is the westernmost section of County Galway, beyond Lough Corrib. Inland are moors and looming hills, lakes and streams fringed by vivid green vegetation, and a massively indented but placid coastline. One main road, the N59, leads through the centre of Connemara and round the northern area, but though scenic enough, it's best to deviate from this for at least part of your travels to take in some of the coast.

Oughterard lies some way inland, but is surprisingly a great fishing centre, serving the resort area of Lough Corrib, Ireland's second largest lake, which virtually splits the county in half. From Oughterard it's worth making the beautiful trip past mirror-like pools to Maam Cross, where the monthly cattle fair is about the only sign of life. Here you can explore the mass of islets along the coastal peninsulas.

Above: fishing with a traditional curragh on the tranquil waters

Left: a boat at rest in the harbour at Roundstone village

The stony remains of an old croft house give this beautiful landscape a touching human scale

The peaceful coastline of Cashel Bay is also recommended . Sheltered from Atlantic gales and storms, this quiet bay sprouts luxuriant subtropical vegetation at every turn.

Roundstone has a particularly attractive setting at the foot of Errisbeg with wonderful views of the Twelve Pins; its tourist industry is taking over from fishing. Cut across the peninsula to see one of the best remaining stretches of Irish blanket bog, now at last recognised as an important ecosystem, rather than something to be dried and burned. It's a lonely road with an uneven camber, so go carefully, especially towards nightfall. The bog is haunted by the ghost of a traveller murdered by two old women who offered him shelter...

THE LAKES

These smallish, watery counties – Cavan and Monaghan near the Northern Ireland border, and Westmeath, Laois, Offaly, Roscommon and Longford – form the geographical heart of Ireland, yet are usually portrayed as places to get through on the way to somewhere more interesting. Closer exploration of these unsung plains is surprisingly rewarding, however, for there are historic towns, abbey ruins and grand houses to visit, and masses of outdoor activities. These central counties also offer a less stereotyped picture of the Emerald Isle. Visitors are welcomed with true Irish hospitality, with no pressure to buy sweaters or shamrock table linen.

The small-scale, piecemeal landscape seems at first monotonous – a shallow saucer of endless arable and pasture land, broken up by a maze of lakes and river systems. Its most significant geographical feature, the River Shannon, is the longest in the British Isles, carving its ponderous course through the brimming flood plains and water meadows of several counties. Laois has the highest hills, the Slieve Blooms, which rise to a modest maximum of 527m. Amid these low-lying plains, however, they seem grand indeed.

Water and sky at Clonmacnoise

Slieve Bloom Mountains

Though not particularly high, the Slieve Blooms rise quite dramatically from the low-lying boggy plains which surround them, their looming purple shoulders a backdrop to many a view in this area. It is said that they are named after Bladhma, an ancient hero, who once took refuge from his enemies in these hills. Later, in turbulent Cromwellian times, the Slieve Blooms again became a place of hiding for men whose lands had been confiscated by the Parliamentary forces.

The slopes are rounded rather than steep, many covered in conifer plantations, and the high density of well-marked paths and tracks (so unusual in Ireland) make them ideal for walking. A long-distance footpath called the Slieve Bloom Way runs for 30km or so around these hills, on a route past waterfalls and glens, through bog and moorland, conifer woods and an ancient (pre-Ice Age) river valley.

Though the hills are mostly too gentle for really dramatic views, the slopes do in some places drop away sufficiently to reveal the great plains below stretching mistily into the distance. Look out for the tracks of the rare pine marten which haunts the mountains, together with Irish hares, fallow deer and mountain goats.

Above: a road sign almost disappears in the bracken, victim of somebody's target practice

Glen Barrow or the standing stone at Forelacka are both good starting points for a walk. Despite their unthreatening altitude (maximum height 527m), these hills can be treacherously misty and waterlogged, so adequate footwear, clothing and equipment are essential.

This low mountain range provides good walking country

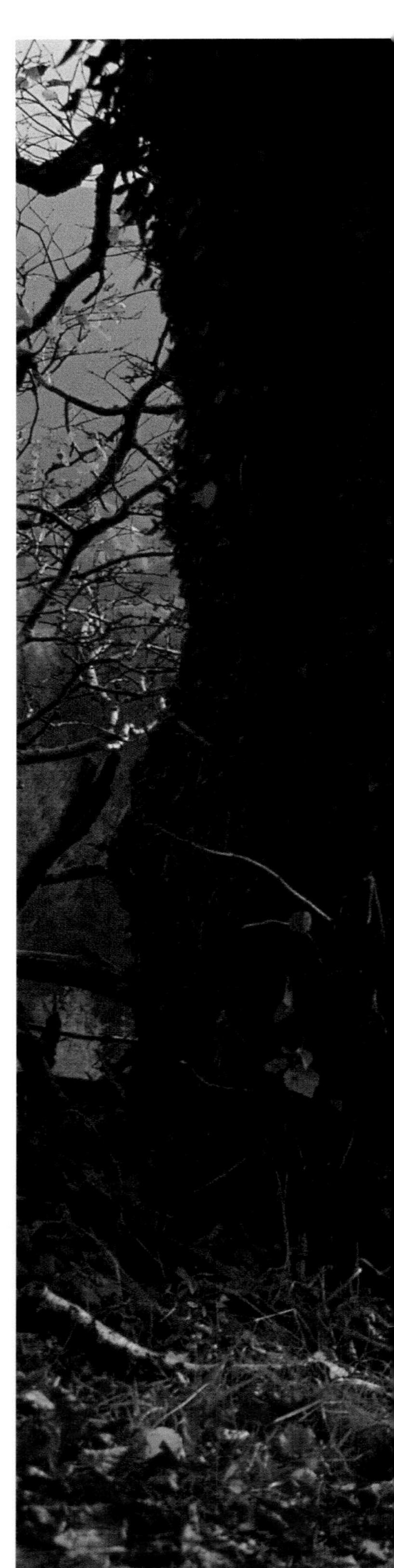

A convenient gate-gap in the hedge provides a rolling vista of the mountains

Below: the site of the old telescope

Birr

This pleasant, quiet Georgian town centres around the attractive Emmet Square; it was formerly known as Parsonstown, after the family name of the Earls of Rosse, whose seat is Birr Castle.

The castle itself is 17th-century Gothic and not generally open to the public, but the 40ha of gardens are open all year and heartily reward a visit. They contain many rare specimen trees and shrubs, including a collection from China, and the

tallest box hedges in the world (10m). The gardens are particularly fine in spring and autumn, when flowering trees, bulbs or colourful foliage are at their best. Walks lead beside the lake and rivers, around which the grounds are landscaped.

The most fascinating feature of Birr Castle, however, is a remarkable early telescope, built locally and recently restored to its former glory. Built by the 3rd Earl of Rosse in the 1840s, it was for many years the largest and most powerful in the world, its 183cm lens enabling the aristocratic astronomer and his son, the 4th Earl, to study the spiral nebulae and measure the heat of the moon. Massive supporting walls once held the long wooden tube of the instrument in place, rigged with a complicated system of ropes and pulleys; taped information today provides background history. The stable block at the castle is home to Ireland's Historic Science Centre, which has exhibitions of astronomy, photography and engineering.

The handsome old castle is set in pleasant gardens

Charleville Forest Castle

Men with great wealth are inclined to indulge in expensive playhouses, and the Gothic Revival Charleville Forest outside the tiny distillery town of Tullamore, County Offaly, is one of the finest of its kind in Europe. It was built by renowned architect Francis Johnston in 1798, and present owners are pleased to show off the secret passages and fantasy dungeons,the extravagance of which hastened the demise of the Bury family fortunes.

The money behind Charleville came from Charles William Bury, a man of wealth and leisure. He had the money to buy himself titles and chunks of history, and was by all accounts a good natured spendthrift. He also enjoyed writing and translating racy verse, and found a wife of tolerant and artistic persuasion. Charleville Forest, full of great and ancient oaks, seemed the perfect setting for a

The Gothic castle is set at the end of a long leafy drive, on extensive lands outside Tullamore

A splendid crystal chandelier hangs above the wooden staircase

medieval-style castle, and the idea for its construction, compete with follies, became an obsessive fancy, taking more than a decade to complete and credited for starting a craze of castle construction amongst the Irish gentry.

However, the Burys had for years been living far beyond their means, and the castle contributed considerably to mounting debt – when Charles died in 1835 the estate was impoverished. Inept heirs did nothing to improve matters, and the castle was shut in the mid-19th century. The last heir, Colonel Howard Charles Bury, is famed for having led the first Everest expedition to find a route through Tibet to the North Col in 1921. He loathed Charleville Castle, however, and sold off its contents in a notorious auction in 1948, after which it sat empty and was nearly destroyed by vandals. Fortunately, however, the new owners have lovingly restored it and the castle is now open to visitors.

The interior of the castle is an enjoyable Gothic fantasy

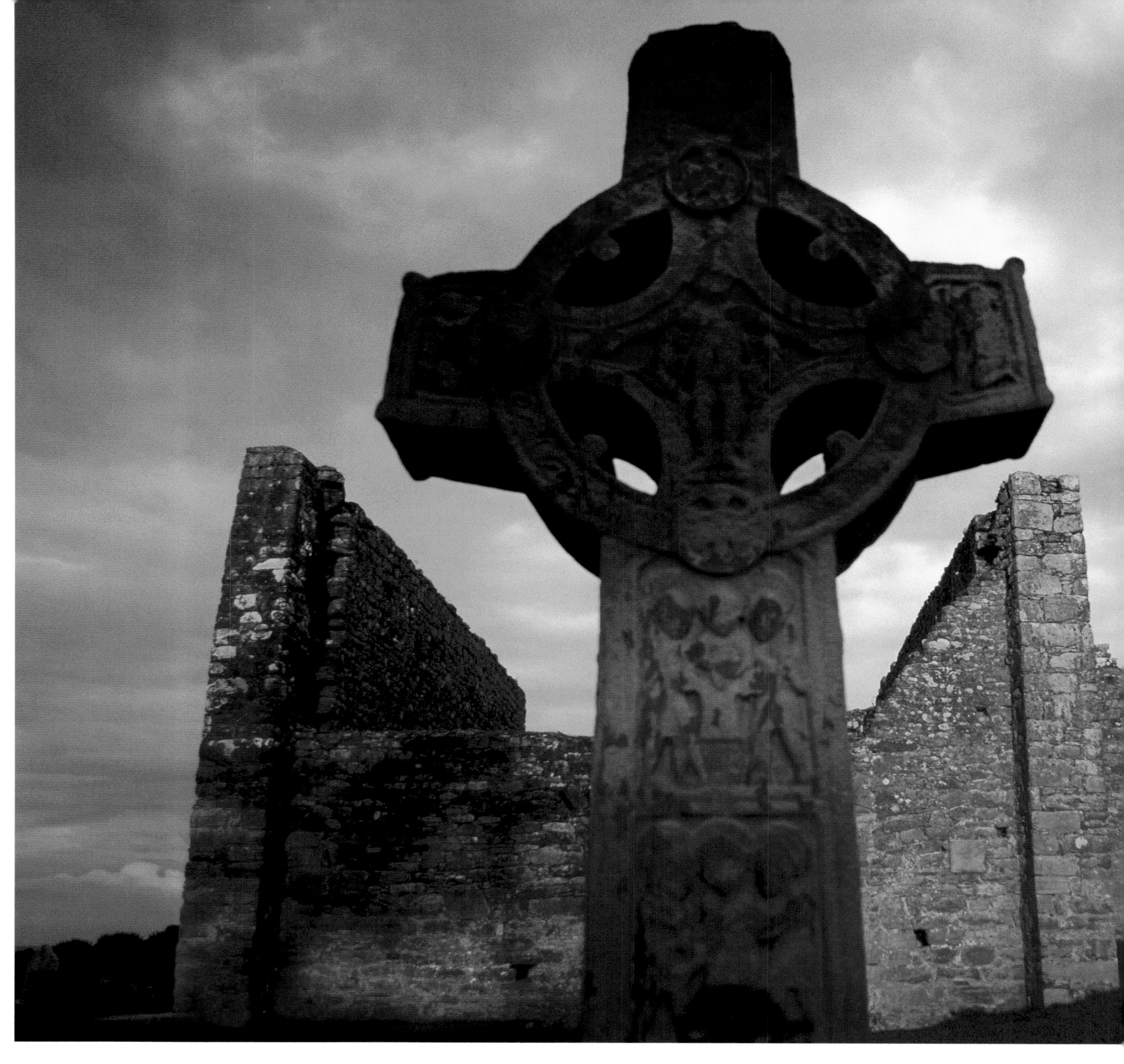

Beautifully interlaced spiral carving on a pillar

The ruins at this important monastic site are remarkably intact, mainly dating from the 12–14th centuries

Clonmacnoise

These extensive and impressive monastic remains stand in velvety, emerald water-meadows by a rushy bend in the River Shannon, a place of almost tangible stillness, especially at dawn or dusk. In earlier centuries it was even more isolated by the river and surrounding bogland, and was accessible only by boat, or along the esker ridge known as the Pilgrims' Causeway.

Founded by St Ciarán (or Kieran) in about AD 548, this Celtic site became the most important religious establishment of its time in Ireland and was renowned as a place of art and learning throughout Europe. St Ciarán himself died of plague at the age of only 33, just seven months after the monastery site had been established, but news of his good works eventually spread beyond Irish shores. Several ecclesiastical treasures from here, including the gold and silver Crozier of Clonmacnoise, are now on display at the National Museum in Dublin. *The Book of the Dun Cow*, one of the earliest and most famous manuscripts in the Irish language, was also produced here.

Clonmacnoise was once a royal city and the burial place of the High Kings of Tara and Connaught, including the last High King, Rory O'Conor. Like most settlements of its type, it suffered constant depredations at the hands of Vikings and Normans and was devastated by English forces in 1552. Still visible within its enclosing walls are the remains of a cathedral, eight churches, two Round Towers, many carved gravestones, and several High Crosses. The most interesting antiquities are displayed in the visitor centre. The splendid Cross of the Scriptures, erected in the 9th or 10th century, depicts, amongst the usual biblical scenes, King Dermot helping St Ciarán erect the first corner-post of the monastery at Clonmacnoise.

The tiny Nuns' Church stands beside a quiet lane outside the main enclosure and is reached via a path through the modern cemetery and out into the road beyond. It was built by Dervorgilla, Ireland's equivalent of Helen of Troy, whose abduction by Dermot MacMurrough provided the excuse for Strongbow's Anglo-Norman invasion.

A round tower stands solid and proud above the surrounding watery landscape

Lough Key

Lough Key marks the northern navigable limit of the meandering River Shannon

A short distance east of Boyle lies the Lough Key Forest Park, part of the Rockingham estate, an enormous demesne which once belonged to the King family (Edward King, drowned in the Irish Sea in 1636, was the subject of Milton's elegiac poem *Lycidas*). Rockingham originally belonged to the MacDermots, the local chieftains and Lords of Moylurg, but was handed to the King family in 1617. The big house in what is now the forest park was burned down in 1957, but King House, the family's town mansion in the main street, can be visited.

Lying in the grounds of the former Rockingham estate, the Lough Key Forest Park ranges over about 340 hectares along a lake shore and includes a cypress grove, deerpark, ice-house, temple, bog garden full of peat-loving plants such as azaleas, and many waymarked paths. Boats tour the lake from Rockingham Harbour, and rowing boats can be hired. There are ring-forts and islands to explore, and a vantage point called the Moylurg Tower can be climbed for views of the surrounding scenery.

Strokestown Park House

Many Irish towns and villages reveal their Georgian origins in wide streets, but Strokestown's is certainly exceptional. Originally modelled on Vienna's Ringstrasse, which had greatly impressed one of the local landowners, it is said to be the widest provincial main street in Ireland. The village is little more than an adjunct to the fine Palladian Strokestown Park House, which lies beyond the Gothic triple arch on this main street. Its most famous (and infamous) proprietor was Major Denis Mahon, who presided over the Strokestown estate during the unproductive Famine years, and found himself so short of cash that he pressed his tenants to emigrate to the New World. Rumours spread that he was chartering the dreaded 'coffin ships' in which so many Irish emigrants perished, and Mahon was shot dead near Strokestown in 1847.

You can hire a little boat from the harbour and row out onto the lake to explore at your own pace

Left: a museum recalling the events of the Famine years occupies a wing of Strokestown Park House

THE NORTHWEST

Donegal's spectacular scenery is often considered the best in Ireland, though its location, tenuously attached to the Republic by a thin isthmus of land between the coast and its severed Ulster neighbours, keeps it remote. Outside a brief, intense summer season, when tourists flit through like butterflies, these northern regions (Counties Sligo, Donegal and Leitrim) can seem forlorn and windswept. All through the year clouds scud rapidly in from the Atlantic, bringing lashing horizontal squalls or drizzling sea-mists. Just as suddenly these are followed by shafts of sunlight and vivid rainbows which alchemise its glens, cliffs, mountains and beaches into the landscapes of holiday brochures. Here, in these far-flung peninsulas, you will find that elusive rural idyll – softly domed ricks of hand-turned hay and whitewashed thatched cottages with scarlet doors. The postcard scene disguises a history of constant struggle against the elements and economic deprivation. There is little industry other than the old cottage-based crafts of knitting and weaving, though these are now organised to catch the tourist's eye in village-like studio complexes.

Clouds pass high above a landscape of rounded drumlins at Carrowkeel

A stone circle of mighty boulders at Carrowmore, its origins lost in the mists of time

Carrowmore

Carrowmore, Carrowkeel and Creevykeel – these confusingly named places are three of the most interesting and important prehistoric sites in the northwestern region.

Carrowmore, not far from the town of Sligo, is the largest group of megalithic burial monuments in the whole of the British Isles, containing the remnants of about 60 tombs, stone circles, dolmens and other antiquities, the earliest of which are alleged to predate the famous passage-grave at Newgrange by about 700 years. Many stones and sites have been damaged or removed over the centuries, and it is incredible to think that in 1983, plans were drawn up – and thankfully abandoned – to turn the site into a rubbish tip.

Carrowkeel, overlooking the well-stocked Lough Arrow in the Bricklieve hills, is an ancient cemetery of circular mounds dating from the late Stone Age (2500–2000 BC). There are some splendid views from the exposed hilltop site.

Creevykeel, near Mullaghmore, is a fine example of a neolithic court-tomb dating from about 3000 BC, with a double burial chamber surrounded by a wedge-shaped mound of stone. Polished stone axes, worked flints and some bronze Celtic artefacts found here are now in the National Museum in Dublin.

Left: an ancient slab-covered tomb at Carrowmore, which would once have been concealed by a mound of stones and earth

Parke's Castle

A fortified manor house with an interestingly chequered history stands by the calm waters of Lough Gill. Built in 1609 by an Ulster settler, Captain Robert Parke, it occupies the site of a much earlier tower-house belonging to the O'Rourke clan, rulers of the kingdom of Breffni. The last unfortunate O'Rourke laird sheltered a shipwrecked Spanish Armada officer and was executed at Tyburn, London, for treason. Features of the medieval structure can be seen in the later house.

Recently the house has been sensitively restored using original materials and local craftsmanship, and it now represents a fascinating piece of research and reconstruction. High walls protect the courtyard. Its witch-hat turrets face the mirror-like lake, and there are splendid views from its ramparts.

Beyond the outer defences near the water's edge lies a little beehive hut of stone. This is a sweat-house, or early Irish sauna, used to alleviate various ailments. From the jetty you can take a boat across the tranquil waters of Lough Gill, set around with hills and attractive forest, calling at the lovely Yeatsian island of Innisfree.

Strong, battlemented walls give the house a sturdy air of fortification

The tree-covered island of Innisfree on Lough Gill was immortalised by W B Yeats in a wistful poem

Sligo

Sligo is one of the largest towns in the Northwest, a lively market town and centre for music, pubs and eating places, designed more for its own 18,000 inhabitants than for tourists. Colourful houses stand alongside the River Garavogue, and the town still has many old quarters and shops of great character. Its literary associations give it a cultural cachet and it now receives a great annual influx of scholars and students on the Yeats trail, especially during August, when a Yeats summer school is held.

Outside the town loom the great hulks of Benbulbin (525m) and Knocknarea (330m), like up-turned ships. Benbulbin is the legendary death-site of Diarmuid, who eloped with Gráinne, and Knocknarea the supposed burial site of Queen Maeve. Both hills may be climbed, but can be treacherous when the mist comes down.

This area is called 'Yeats Country'' as the poet passed much of his childhood and was eventually buried here, though his adult life was largely spent in Dublin, and in Galway at Thoor Ballylee or at Coole Park. Off the N15 north of Sligo, Yeats's tomb lies in Drumcliff churchyard. Further up the same road, follow the coastal turning to Lissadell House, 19th-century home of the Gore-Booth family. Sisters Eva Gore-Booth and Constance Markiewicz, friends of Yeats, took part in the Easter Rising. The house, in need of restoration, is surrounded by rampant vegetation.

The curious flat-topped bulk of Benbulbin was a source of inspiration to the poet

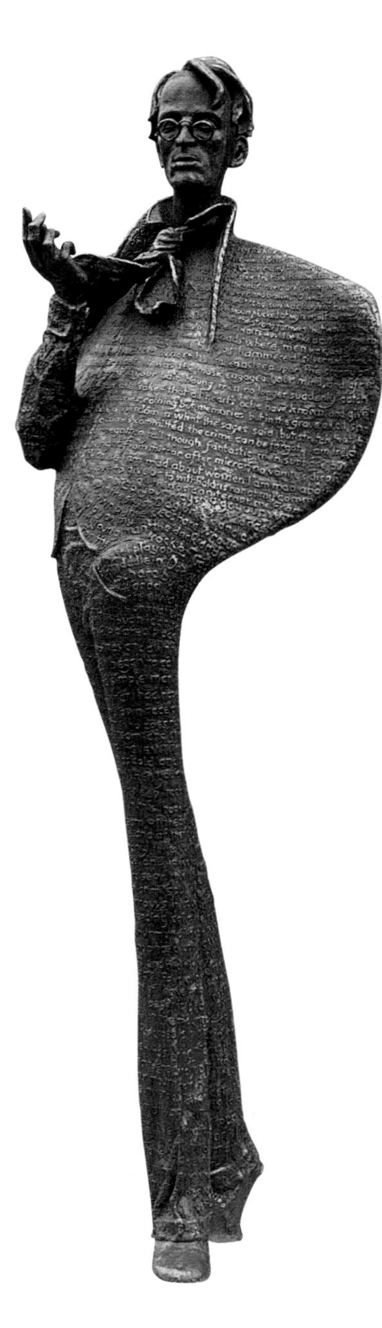

Above: this famous languid statue of W B Yeats (1865–1939), covered in verse, stands in Sligo town centre

Left: Yeats was a frequent guest at Lissadell House

Glenveagh National Park

Ten thousand hectares of wild scenery make up this park of glaciated valleys and open moorland around Lough Veagh. Parts of the park are wooded with native oak and birch or imported rhododendron and spruce. The approach via Dunlewy at the foot of Mount Errigal gives some of the most spectacular views. (Off the main road, an expedition to the Poisoned Glen is worth taking – it is so called because of a toxic variety of spurge which grows by the waterside.)

Beside Lough Veagh stands the estate of Glenveagh Castle, created during the mid-19th century by John George Adair, who built the romantic, Scottish-style castellated mansion in about 1870. He is remembered mostly for the harsh eviction of all his tenants after the murder of one of his estate managers in 1861. Adair later emigrated to North America. His wife Cornelia left much more favourable impressions: returning to Glenveagh after her husband's death, she created the 11 hectares of glorious gardens around the castle.

During the Civil War the castle was occupied by the IRA and the Free State Army, then restored by a benevolent American owner who later transferred the land to the Irish National Parks Service. The estate contains the largest herd of red deer in Ireland, believed to number about 600.

Surrounded by low mountains, Lough Veagh forms the focus of the national park

John George Adair's romantic castle by the lough

A patchwork of farmland and sea at Ballyness Bay, near Bloody Foreland

Sheep occupy a quiet road through the bog

A calm sea off the Bloody Foreland, which takes its name from the hue of the local stone rather than any colourful event in history

Bloody Foreland

Despite its tragic sounding name, reminiscent of battle grounds from Ireland's turbulent history, the Bloody Foreland (*Cnoc Fola*) is a beauty spot which earned its title from the ruby and flame hues reflected from its granite cliffs, especially vibrant at sunset when the color bleeds into the sea. Just off shore lie Inishbofin, Inishdooey and Inishbeg, largely uninhabited today, but the more distant Tory island still maintains an independent community of lobster fishermen and has been inhabited since prehistoric times. In ancient Irish legend Tory was the residence of Balor, the one-eyed Celtic god of Darkness, who seems to have been fitted with a laser beam in order to strike down his enemies. More recently it was home to monks of St Columba. Wrapped in amethyst mists, it is easy to see how such a spot could acquire a reputation for magic from the shore, and certain ancient beliefs still abound there, such as those of the 'Cursing Stones' which helped drive away unwanted visitors.

Horn Head (*Corran Binne*, or 'Hollow in the Hills') is a sheer quartzite cliff at the northernmost tip of the peninsula, which plunges 180m into the Atlantic ocean and affords spectacular views in good weather. It is also home to many colonies of seabirds, including the cartoon-like puffin with its bright orange beak, and their laments echo against the crashing surf below.

Grianán of Aileach

This remarkable circular fortress lies about 14km south of Buncrana, perched on a hilltop and reached by a small winding lane. Aerial photographs of it (see opposite) show the stone ring-fort in an emerald pool of grassland amid scrubby tufts of brownish heather and gorse. The name means 'stone palace of the sun'. Similar cashel forts can be seen elsewhere in Ireland, such as Staigue Fort in County Kerry. The precise age of this fort is disputed, some authorities dating it well before the Christian era (to about 1700 BC), others rather later. Its presence was recorded by Ptolemy in the 2nd century AD, and it was used as a stronghold by the O'Neill kings for several centuries before its gradual destruction.

Its suspiciously neat appearance is due to enthusiastic restoration during the 1870s by Dr Walter Bernard, an amateur historian from Derry. The round enclosure measures about 23m across, with walls over 5m high

The circular hilltop fort is open to the skies

and 4m thick. A single gate allows access to the interior, which contains four tiers of steps and various passages or storage places.

If you are lucky enough to visit it on a fine day, the views from this hilltop are amazing, stretching for huge distances over Derry, the Fanad and Inishowen peninsulas, and the Swilly estuary.

Inside, steps lead up the tiers of the great wall, with fantastic panoramic views from the top

An aerial view clearly shows the concentric rings of the construction

The weather reports from Malin Head provide critical information for crews of the fishing boats

Inishowen Peninsula

Ireland's most northerly point lies in the Republic on this ragged triangular headland, not in Northern Ireland as most people would expect. Lough Foyle and Lough Swilly virtually isolate Inishowen from the rest of the county. The interior is a mix of low white farms and cottages huddling against the wind, and grand brown mountains rising toward Slieve Snaght. The scenic 160km route around the edge of Inishowen takes in Malin Head, castles, churches, High Crosses and pre-Christian antiquities.

Buncrana is the main centre, a popular holiday resort much favoured by inhabitants of Derry. Throughout the centuries it witnessed many clashes between English and Irish. Ireland's remote extremities were always feared (not without reason) as a potential Achilles' heel in English defences against invading Catholic forces from Spain or

France, and any hints of disaffection were dealt with ruthlessly. In 1602 the O'Dohertys prepared to welcome a second Spanish Armada here and a couple of centuries later rebel Wolfe Tone was held in Buncrana Castle.

Malin is a 17th-century plantation village built around a green, its most striking feature a long bridge of stone arches. Malin Head relays weather reports from the fishing village of Ballyhillin, sheltered from the worst of the storms by the rocky promontory.

Above: a long strip of white sandy beach at Portnod

Left: almost the end of the road at Malin Head, Ireland's most northerly point

NORTHERN IRELAND

For many years, the Troubles have been a significant factor in any decision to visit Northern Ireland, but Northern Ireland is, most of the time, in most places, as tranquil as anywhere in the South – and that makes it pretty quiet. Outside the trouble spots, Northern Ireland feels, and is, entirely peaceful, and wherever they come from, visitors receive a warm welcome. Local people are anxious to show outsiders the good side of the province and, whether Catholic or Protestant, are extraordinarily hospitable. The vast majority of people are simply interested in getting on with their lives in peace.

The scenery of Northern Ireland is its primary attraction, and most of its appeal is concentrated in a few clearly defined rural areas: the Mountains of Mourne; the Glens of Antrim; the Causeway Coast; and the Lakes of Fermanagh. The Ulster Way is one of the best long-distance footpaths in Ireland, leading through the province's most scenic and beautiful landscapes. But it is the cities of the North, especially Belfast and Derry, that give a complete picture and these cannot be ignored if you want to see more than the surface prettiness.

Hexagonal basalt columns make an irregular pavement beside the sea at the Giant's Causeway

Glens of Antrim

The glens of Antrim and the surrounding coast from Larne to Bushmills contain some of the most beautiful and spectacular scenery in Northern Ireland. Originally intended for military use, the coast road which hugs the shoreline was completed in the 1830s and now provides an artery along which travellers can experience the long history of war, settlement and religion.

Travelling northwards, the village of Glenarm signals the start of the nine glens of Antrim, all worth exploring, each with its own special charm and character. Glencloy – the 'glen of hedges' – is the next, with the terraced houses of Carnlough resolutley facing the sea. The road north continues to follow the coast, with the hills behind rising up to the Antrim Plateau, 350m. Behind the sleepy village of Cushendall lies the Stone Age axe factory at Tievebulliagh, where there is a plentiful supply of porcellanite, a hard, tough, bluish-grey rock. This is such a rare rock type that you can be fairly certain that any porcellanite blade found in the British Isles comes from County Antrim.

The picturesque ruins of Layd Church are worth a detour in Glencorp. A neolithic court tomb at Cushendall, the romantically named Ossian's Grave, provides a fantastic viewpoint looking out to Glendun, Glenaan and even to Scotland. The scenic road continues round Murlough Bay and the spectacular cliffs of Fair Head, all the way to Bushmills on the north coast.

Right: an aerial view of pretty Cushenden village shows the glen stretching behind and inland

Right: the inlet at Glenarm

A sparkling waterfall in the forest park at Glenariff

the Leeds
LOCAL AGENCY
The Galley
RESTAURANT
Derry
Craft
Village
Restaurant
Galley
ROARING
MEG
Pottery Portraits
We can glaze your
photographs onto
wall plaques or
plates.

Derry

This historic city, in the county of Londonderry, is now officially known by its original name of Derry, although its Loyalist population still refers to it as Londonderry (an allusion to James I's gift of the city to the livery companies of London). Derry's notorious Bogside district has seen much unrest, for it is here that Catholic/Protestant tribalism is most sharply polarised. Catholics, unwillingly stranded right on the Republic's border, have suffered much discrimination under gerrymandered Protestant control, while Loyalists find it impossible to cast off their atavistic siege mentality. On a free-standing gable-end near the Bogside (once an IRA no-go area and the scene of 'Bloody Sunday', when 13 Catholic civilians were killed in 1972 during a civil rights march) are the giant words 'You are now entering Free Derry'. Protestants reply a few streets away with the defiant slogan 'No Surrender'.

For all its political ill-feelings, Derry is a fascinating city, retaining intact the 17th-century walls that have played such a significant role in its history. These sturdy ramparts, 8m high and up to 9m thick, have never been breached. Five of the cannons that defended the city during its long siege stand above Shipgate Quay. Walkways lead along parts of the city walls, giving excellent views of both the inner city and the lower city with its great modern bridge spanning the Foyle.

Within the walls are an extraordinary little enclave of old-fashioned shops and bars, the Protestant cathedral of St Columb in 'Planters' Gothic' style and a typical Ulster central square known as the Diamond. A hopeful sign of constructive community spirit is the Derry Craft Village where modern artisanry burgeons in a village-like complex, and a pleasant coffee shop called The Boston Tea Party provides an excuse for a sit-down.

Vivid street artwork highlights local differences

A coat of arms displays the red hand of Ulster

The square known as the Diamond is the hub of the modern city

Pleasantly leafy Shipquay Street, with the entrance to the Derry Craft Village

Looking along the cliffs from Carrick-a-Rede

The Giant's Causeway

This extraordinary phenomenon is Northern Ireland's most famous landmark, first brought to public attention in 1693 by the Royal Geographical Society. Visitors have flocked here from far and wide ever since. The site is on a cliff-lined coast of outstanding natural beauty and is now in the care of the National Trust.

The Giant's Causeway is a complex series of promontories, but the most spectacular section consists of about 37,000 polygonal columns of dark basalt, many tawny with lichen, packed so neatly together that it is easy to imagine them as building blocks of some supernatural hand. Most columns are hexagonal, forming a honeycomb pattern, but some have five, seven or as many as ten sides. They measure about 30cm across and may reach a height of 12m. Besides the classic 'threepenny-bit' stacks there are other weird and wonderful formations, some like bulbous eyes, others like ramparts. All were formed about 55 million years ago, after a volcanic eruption caused molten basalt to pour out above the chalky bedrock, crystallising into these regular structures as it cooled. Legends have arisen about the origins of the Causeway; the main one tells how the Ulster giant, Finn MacCool, built it to walk across to Scotland.

At the top of the cliffs, a large modern visitor centre contains an interesting exhibition about the Causeway and the local history and wildlife. During high season a little minibus shuttles visitors down the steep path to the rocks, but the best way to enjoy the spectacle is to walk along the North Antrim Cliff Path towards Carrick-a-rede. And even out of season, when no other visitors are around and the waves crash on these bleak, dark rocks, the Causeway is a magical place.

Along the cliffs, tall columns of stone rise up like gigantic organ pipes

Below: an unusual density of basalt columns gives this entirely natural phenomenon its name

AEQUORA
VENTIS

Mussenden Temple

Downhill House, near Coleraine, was the residence of the eccentric Anglican Bishop Frederick Augustus Hervey, fourth Earl of Bristol, a descendent of a long line of rascals. Derry was one of the wealthiest of Ireland's church districts and it was here Earl-Bishop Hervey reigned at the end of the 18th century, always managing to wrest the maximum from his see in order to live extravagantly and indulge odd whims, such as a 'curate's race' along the beach of Downhill, where the winners were rewarded with positions in the diocese. He also had a passion for travelling the Continent with a massive carriage and entourage, making him so popular with hoteliers that 'Bristol' was often added to the name for status.

Four architects were employed for the construction of the Downhill estate, reflecting the Earl-Bishop's mercurial temperament, and though a fire in 1851 destroyed most of the mansion, numerous 'follies' around the grounds still stand in corny magnificence. One such, Mussenden Temple, is a rotunda with Corinthian columns, closely modelled on the Italian Temples of Vesta. Built in 1783 by Michael Shanahan, the Temple was later named as a memorial for the Bishop's beloved second cousin, Fridiswide Bruce Mussenden, who died at the age of 22. The Temple also served as the Bishop's library, and an occasional church, commanding a spectacular view over the six mile long Atlantic beach.

Delicate swags and relief adorn the stonework of this curious tower

The building stands in splendid isolation, perilously close to the ever-encroaching cliff

Ulster Folk and Transport Museum

This superb museum collection is located about 8km east of Belfast in the extensive grounds of Cultra Manor on the Bangor road. Typical Ulster buildings have been re-erected or reconstructed here and furnished in turn-of-the-century style. The fascinating exhibits include whole urban terraces, shops and cottages, farmhouses, a flax mill, a forge and even a school. Live farm animals and costumed actors bring the whole place to life. Inside, you can watch demonstrations of local crafts such as spinning and weaving, while outside you may see activities such as ploughing and thatching. An entertaining exhibition of domestic, social and agricultural life in Ulster can be seen in the gallery which functions as an introduction to the park.

The transport galleries, found on the opposite side of the main road, house the entire Belfast Transport Museum, and include a fascinating range of exhibits, from horse-drawn carts to the notoriously ill-fated De Lorean sports car. The Irish Railway Collection, with its steam engines and videos, is one of the best sections of this museum. Local engineering heroes, such as Harry Ferguson, receive due attention, as do the great Belfast transport firms such as Shorts, the aircraft manufacturers, and Harland & Wolff, the shipbuilders (one of their most famous commissions was the *Titanic*).

Above: a whole street of terraces in the park

Right: inside, the houses are simply furnished, complete with a reeking peat fire to keep out the damp

A display of two-wheeled motoring history in the complementary Transport Museum

It seems quite natural to see a horse and cart outside the reconstructed cottages

Belfast

Since Partition, Belfast has been the official capital of Northern Ireland. It is not the seat of government, however; Northern Ireland has been ruled directly from Westminster since 1972, and despite a recent re-opening of the Northern Ireland Parliament at Stormont, its authority has been suspended at the time of writing.

With a population of around 400,000, Belfast is much smaller than Dublin, and an exodus of the younger middle-classes during the past two decades to dormitory towns and suburbs has unbalanced the city centre's demography, though it is still a transient home for over 8,000 university students. Apart from its two best museums, none of its sights is hugely compelling, but the city has a highly distinctive atmosphere and there is plenty to occupy a pleasant day or two.

Perhaps few people unfamiliar with the city will immediately warm to the prospect of a stay here. Religious bigotry, sectarian violence and deliberately high-profile security measures have in the past given the impression to outsiders that Northern Ireland's capital is a war-zone.

Like many things in Ireland, however, the reality is a surprise. If anything, Belfast is less of a risk for the average visitor than Dublin. Security checks and searches (much less stringent since the 1994 ceasefire) are endured with the stoicism that prevailed during World War II, when Belfast's dockyard targets caused many civilian casualties. Despite

The grand classical Belfast City Hall stands at the hub of the city

security alerts, the show goes on. Indeed, Belfast hosts one of Britain's liveliest and most acclaimed arts festivals at Queen's University each November, as well as an impressive year-round series of concerts, exhibitions, opera and drama. Restaurants along its Golden Mile bustle, and sports events flourish.

The great engineering works that once made Belfast so prosperous are in sad decline and unemployment figures in the province are among the highest in the UK. Its earliest

The great yellow cranes of Harland and Wolff still dominate the dock area

Far left: the superb modern concert hall overlooks the waterfront

The modern shopping centre of Castle Court thrives along the pedestrianised Royal Avenue

industries included rope-making and linen, cotton spinning and printing. In 1859 the UK's largest shipyards were established here by the Yorkshire engineer Edward Harland and a marine draughtsman from Hamburg, Gustav Wilhelm Wolff. Two vast yellow cranes with the initials 'H & W' painted on them still dominate the dockland skyline as powerfully as any cathedral and are affectionately known as Samson and Goliath.

Other industrial firms closely associated with Belfast are Shorts, the aircraft manufacturers, and Gallahers, the tobacco giant.

Belfast's setting is often praised more than the city itself. The name derives from the Gaelic *beal feirste*, meaning 'mouth of the sandy ford', and Belfast stands proudly at the head of a deep sea-lough surrounded by unspoilt hills, the River Lagan cutting through its heart. The city has abundant parks and open spaces. Within minutes, fast roads take you beyond the outskirts to scenic areas like the Ards Peninsula or Strangford Lough; it is a slightly longer journey to the Mountains of Mourne or the Glens of Antrim.

The city's commercial centre and university area lie close to the river on its western side; prosperous residential

Right: a mural with a message of hope on the Falls Road

The imposing frontage of the parliament building, Stormont, first opened in 1932

districts are to the east and south. On the far west of town, beyond the dividing pale of the Westlink motorway, are the notorious sectarian ghettos that have given the city its worst reputation. The overcrowded, run-down areas of Ballymurphy, Falls and Shankill are depressing, but to some they are oddly fascinating, and visitors will venture there to see the vivid and sometimes highly artistic displays of street mural propaganda (both Catholic and Protestant varieties, incidentally, may be carried out by the same artist!).
The Peace Line is a barricade of iron dividing Protestant and Catholic areas.

Stormont

On the A20, 7km east, is Stormont, a grand, classical building, once again housing the Northern Ireland Parliament. It stands proudly at the top of a sweeping drive through neat parkland. The Scottish baronial Stormont Castle near by contains the office of the Northern Ireland Secretary of State. Both can be viewed only from outside for obvious reasons.

Ulster-American Folk Park

This living history park near Omagh, County Tyrone, has been set up with a generous endowment by the Mellon banking magnates who founded Pittsburgh, Pennsylvania. Thomas Mellon left Ulster in 1818 with his family and became vastly prosperous. The park has been constructed in the peaty bogs around his birthplace at Camphill, a modest, whitewashed cottage, and traces the progress of those early Ulster émigrés from the Old World to the New.

A guided walk takes visitors from a large reception and exhibition centre through birch groves. In the first section, reconstructed buildings create the atmosphere of a typical 18th-century Ulster village, with a blacksmith's forge, a weaver's cottage, and a dour Presbyterian meeting house where interminable sermons were preached. Costumed staff

Patchwork is just one of the skills the Irish emigrants took with them

cook up griddle cakes over open peat fires, spin wool and organise 'lessons' in the village school (quill pens are used).

One of the more imposing buildings is Hugh Campbell's house, where extracts from the journal of 1818, written during his emigration voyage, can be read: 'During the night every moveable in the ship was put in motion by the great heaving ... buckets full of all kinds of filth were hurled in the greatest confusion through the steerage to the great offence of our smelling organs!' On 12 July he wrote, 'This day the anniversary of the Battle of the Boyne was commemorated by a certain part of our passengers to the no small annoyance of another part,' which suggests that not much has changed in the intervening years.

Visitors then pass through the Emigration Gallery, a replica emigration ship (complete with sound effects of creaking timbers and roaring seas) and on to the New World, where typical log barns, wagons and farmsteads of the early settlers can be seen. Of its type this theme park is highly successful and has a coherent and authentic ring.

Above: a glimpse inside a reconstructed pioneer's cottage gives an impression of comfort and cosiness

A pioneer encampment and early log cabin on the New World side of the park

Cruising the gentle waters of Lough Erne

Lough Erne

The appealing little town of Enniskillen owes much of its attractiveness to its setting on an island where the two sections of Lough Erne constrict to their narrowest point. Several routes converge on Enniskillen's strategic location and at busy times it can be a traffic bottleneck. Nevertheless, it makes a good base for exploring Fermanagh's lakeland, where boat trips, fishing and several islands offer many diversions.

In the town the main places of interest are the quaintly turreted Watergate, and the castle, which contains two museums. One is a heritage centre devoted to Fermanagh life and customs, the other a museum dedicated to the Royal Inniskilling Fusiliers and Dragoons. The town's military associations with these famous regiments have made it a terrorist target. In 1987 Enniskillen suffered one of the

Above: the solid bastion of Enniskillen's defensive Watergate

Left: fine detail on the lid of a Belleek Pottery dish

IRA's most violent assaults, when a Remembrance Day ceremony was bombed; 11 people were killed, 61 injured.

Boat trips operate from various points on Lower Lough Erne (the northern lake), where several islands can be visited. Boa Island, White Island and Devenish Island all have interesting Celtic or early Christian antiquities. Reached via the pretty lake-shore roads, Castle Archdale Country Park and Castle Caldwell Forest Park offer good woodland walks and picnic sites.

At the far western tip of the lake, straddling the border with the Republic, Belleek is famous for its pottery. Guided tours around the factory can be arranged and a museum and visitor centre display some of its wares. Belleek pottery is extraordinarily elaborate and delicate; clay is extruded in thin strands which are then laid over each other in complex lattice patterns to form the classic 'basketware' style. With such an intricate and delicate process, it is perhaps no surprise that the results are not cheap.

Castle Coole and Florence Court

The grand Palladian mansion of Castle Coole, home of the Earls of Belmore, is the most impressive house of its age in Ireland. Its original cost was enormous (furnishing it was even more expensive than its construction) and it has recently been faithfully restored, at vast expense, by the National Trust.

A masterpiece by James Wyatt, completed in 1798, the house contains magnificent plasterwork and curved doors of ancient mahogany. It is perhaps more of a showpiece than its neighbour, Florence Court.

Florence Court

This is another particularly fine mid-18th-century Palladian house. The seat of the Earls of Enniskillen, it was superbly restored after a disastrous fire in 1956. Splendid plasterwork is the main feature, best preserved on the staircase and dining-room ceiling, which quick-thinking workmen saved from collapse during the fire by drilling holes to drain flood water. The house has a relaxed, lived-in air.

It is an unusual claim to fame, but every example of the Irish-type yew tree ultimately comes from cuttings taken from a mutant discovered in the gardens of Florence Court. The branches have an distinguishing upright habit instead of the normal spreading growth. The original tree was identified and first propagated in 1767, and the Irish yew is now planted widely in graveyards and formal gardens.

Right: a harp adorns one corner of the comfortable library, Castle Coole

Above: magnificent plasterwork in the entrance hall, Florence Court

Right: the splendid porticoed front of Castle Coole

A game of road bowls holds up the traffic

Below: the view from the Roman Catholic cathedral takes in the square tower of its Protestant rival

Armagh

Armagh has often been the scene of battle: County Armagh is predominantly Catholic, especially in the south, but the city itself is a Protestant stronghold. The two rival cathedrals, both dedicated to St Patrick, scowl at each other from two of Armagh's seven small hills. The Protestant one is kept locked for security reasons, but instructions for obtaining the key are posted on the door. Solid, squat and square, it is mostly 19th century in perpendicular Gothic style, with a fringe of grotesque heads around its otherwise plain exterior. It is the burial place of Brian Ború, the warlike king who finally drove the Vikings out of Ireland. The Roman Catholic cathedral, completed in 1873, stands proudly twin-spired at the top of a long flight of steps. The interior is astonishingly ornate – walls and roof covered with rich mosaics of saints and angels.

The Mall, a broad, tree-lined square, is surrounded by some of Armagh's finest Georgian buildings, including the courthouse and the Royal Irish Fusiliers and County Museums. The town's most unusual sights are the 18th-century Observatory and neighbouring Planetarium, where computer displays and models track down heavenly bodies. They stand in a park specially laid out to show the relationships of the planets. Navan Fort, now just a huge mound to the west, was the ancient palace of Queen Macha, a site which rivalled Tara, and the court of Ulster's chivalrous Red Branch Knights.

The ancient game of road bowls is played along the local roads around the city (a version of it can also be seen in Schull, County Cork). A heavy iron ball about the size of a cricket ball is hurled along the lanes, and the aim is to reach the end of the winding 4km course in the fewest number of throws. Betting is fierce. Ask for details in local pubs if you want to see a game – most take place on Sunday afternoons, and the first Sunday in August is championship day.

The twin spires and twin gateposts of Armagh's Victorian Roman Catholic cathdral

Mount Stewart

Mount Stewart House itself is richly furnished 18th-century mansion, stuffed with interesting objects, including a magnificent painting by Stubbs, and marble statues and political memorabilia. It was built as the home of the Marquess of Londonderry. Viscount Castlereagh, the politician who signed the Act of Union of 1801 linking Ireland with Britain, was actually born here in 1769, and nearly drowned in the lough as a teenager.

The magnificent grounds cover some 35 hectares, encompassing woods, lakes and formal gardens

The gardens are the outstanding feature at Mount Stewart, and were created by the Edith, wife of the 7th Marquis of Londonderry, during the 1920s. The mild microclimate engendered by neighbouring Strangford Lough enables many rare and tender plants to flourish here, and there's lots to explore, including lakes and woods. The gardens are now in the care of the National Trust. James Stuart's graceful octagonal Classical folly overlooking the lough, called theTemple of the Winds, echoes a similar structure in Athens.

Below: beautiful proportions in the hall and gallery, Mount Stewart

Sunset over the lough, near Ardmillan

Strangford Lough

The great expanse of Strangford Lough on Ireland's northeast coast is almost choked off from the sea by the narrow channel at Portaferry. The tides rush through here with particular force, separating the tip of the long, narrow finger of the Ards Peninsula from the mainland shore. It's a popular lake for sailing and watersports.

The lake is also an important wildlife and wetland habitat, supporting colonies of seals as well as numerous seabirds on its rich mudflats, particularly waders. Winter visitors include the distinctive pied eider ducks, and thousands of noisy Brent geese. There's a great diversity of marine plant- and wildlife under the water, too, and you can find out more details about this remarkable ecosystem in the aquarium, Exploris,near the quayside at Portaferry, which is devoted to local marine life.

Castle Ward

On the shores of Strangford Lough is Castle Ward, a mansion which clearly displays the diverse tastes of its 18th-century owners, Lord and Lady Bangor. He liked Classical style, while she favoured Gothic. Architecture was not all they disagreed on and eventually they separated. Despite its bizarre disparity of styles, the house and contents are of great interest, giving a vivid impression of Victorian life (see the laundry and the playroom). Within the 280ha estate are a 17th-century tower-house, a wildfowl collection and an exhibition about Strangford Lough.

The little car ferry plies the narrow neck of the lough at Portaferry

Mountains of Mourne

These wild, steep-sided granite hills present an unforgettable aspect. They reach to an average height of about 600m and are largely inaccessible except on foot, though the range is ringed by roads.

If you want to explore the Mourne area, stay in the delightful village of Carlingford over the border in the Republic, or choose one of the eastern coastal resorts. Newcastle is the main tourist centre for the mountains. The resort, though pleasantly set, is of no great interest, but it has a wonderful sandy beach. There are good walks in the nearby forest parks of Tollymore and Castlewellan.

Slieve Donard is the highest Mourne peak at 852m and it is said that on rare, clear days you can see all the countries of the British Isles from its summit (a relatively safe and easy climb). You will also find a hermit cell up there. At one time the mountains were a remote and ungovernable area inhabited by smugglers. A maze of ancient tracks leads through open moorland and upland pasture, which make excellent walking country. Rock-climbing is popular on the steeper cliff faces.

The most accessible section is a well-marked tourist route called the Silent Valley which leads up to two reservoirs serving the Greater Belfast region. A visitor centre stands here and shuttle buses take tourists from the car park to Ben Crom Reservoir (other traffic is banned).

The upper sections of the Mourne hills are characterised by tiny fields and dry-stone walls. The Mourne Wall is the largest of these, 35km long and 2m high, built to give employment to local labour, and enclosing the water catchment area around the Silent Valley. Many semi-precious stones have been mined in the slopes around Hare's Gap.

Far left: the mountains were immortalised in the 19th century in a sentimental song

The Mountains of Mourne form a perfect backdrop to the wide sands along the shore at Newcastle

Acknowledgements

The Automobile Association wishes to thank the following Photo Libraries and photographers for their assistance in the preparation of this book.

Simon McBride was commissioned to take photographs for this publication.

1 BORD FAILTE/IRISH TOURIST BOARD; 2/3 SLIDEFILE; 6/7 SLIDEFILE; 8/9 AA PHOTO LIBRARY (Simon McBride); 10 AA PHOTO LIBRARY (Stephen Whitehorne); 10/11 AA PHOTO LIBRARY (Simon McBride); 11 AA PHOTO LIBRARY; Simon McBride; 12/13 AA PHOTO LIBRARY; 13(t) AA PHOTO LIBRARY (Simon McBride); 13(b) AA PHOTO LIBRARY (Michael Short); 14 AA PHOTO LIBRARY (Simon McBride);14/15 AA PHOTO LIBRARY (Simon McBride); 16(l) AA PHOTO LIBRARY (Stephen Whitehorn); 16(tr) AA PHOTO LIBRARY (Stephen Whitehorne); 16(br) AA PHOTO LIBRARY (Simon McBride); 17 AA PHOTO LIBRARY (Simon McBride); 18/19 AA PHOTO LIBRARY (Simon McBride); 19(t) AA PHOTO LIBRARY (Simon McBride); 19(b) AA PHOTO LIBRARY (Simon McBride); 20/21CHRISTOPHER HILL PHOTOGRAPHIC LIBRARY; 22 SLIDEFILE; 22/23 SLIDEFILE; 24/25 SLIDEFILE; 25 AA PHOTO LIBRARY (Chris Coe); 26/27 SLIDEFILE; 27(t) NATIONAL MUSEUM OF IRELAND; 27(b) AA PHOTO LIBRARY (Michael Short); 28 AA PHOTO LIBRARY (Michael Short); 28/29 SLIDEFILE; 29 SLIDEFILE; 30 (l) AA PHOTO LIBRARY (Simon McBride); 30(r) AA PHOTO LIBRARY (Simon McBride); 30/31 AA PHOTO LIBRARY (Simon McBride); 31 AA PHOTO LIBRARY (Simon McBride); 32 AA PHOTO LIBRARY (Simon McBride); 32/33 AA PHOTO LIBRARY (Simon McBride); 33(t) TREVOR JONES THOROUGHBRED PHOTOGRAPHY; 33(b) TREVOR JONES THOROUGHBRED PHOTOGRAPHY; 34/35 SLIDEFILE; 35 AA PHOTO LIBRARY (Michael Short); 36 AA PHOTO LIBRARY (Chris Coe); 36/37 SLIDEFILE; 37 SLIDEFILE; 38/39 AA PHOTO LIBRARY (Simon McBride); 40 AA PHOTO LIBRARY (Simon McBride); 40/41 AA PHOTO LIBRARY (Simon McBride); 41(t) AA PHOTO LIBRARY (Michael Short); 41(b) AA PHOTO LIBRARY (Simon McBride); 42 SLIDEFILE; 43(l) AA PHOTO LIBRARY (Steve Day); 43(r) Christopher J. Wilson (Wexford Wildfowl Reserve); 44/45 AA PHOTO LIBRARY (Michael Short); 45 AA PHOTO LIBRARY (Michael Short); 46 SLIDEFILE; 47(l) WATERFORD CRYSTAL (Terry Murphy); 47(tr) WATERFORD CRYSTAL (Terry Murphy); 47(br) AA PHOTO LIBRARY (Michael Short); 48 (t) AA PHOTO LIBRARY (Simon McBride); 48(b) AA PHOTO LIBRARY (Simon McBride); 49 AA PHOTO LIBRARY (Simon McBride); 50/51 AA PHOTO LIBRARY (Simon McBride); 51 AA PHOTO LIBRARY (Simon McBride); 52(l) AA PHOTO LIBRARY (Simon McBride); 52(r) AA PHOTO LIBRARY (Simon McBride); 52/53 AA PHOTO LIBRARY (Simon McBride); 54 AA PHOTO LIBRARY (Stephen Hill); 54/55 SLIDEFILE; 55 AA PHOTO LIBRARY (Jamie Blandford); 56/57 AA PHOTO LIBRARY (Jamie Blandford); 58 SKYSCAN (John Eagle); 58/59 AA PHOTO LIBRARY (Jamie Blandford); 59 SLIDEFILE; 60 AA PHOTO LIBRARY (Stephen Hill); 61 AA PHOTO LIBRARY (Jamie Blandford); 62/63 AA PHOTO LIBRARY (Jamie Blandford); 63(t) AA PHOTO LIBRARY (Simon McBride); 63(b) AA PHOTO LIBRARY (Simon McBride); 64 AA PHOTO LIBRARY (Simon McBride); 65 AA PHOTO LIBRARY (Simon McBride); 66/67 AA PHOTO LIBRARY (Simon McBride); 67 AA PHOTO LIBRARY (Simon McBride); 68/69 SLIDEFILE; 69(t) AA PHOTO LIBRARY (Stephen Hill); 69(b) SKYSCAN („KEVIN DWYER); 70(l) AA PHOTO LIBRARY (Jamie Blandford); 70(r) AA PHOTO LIBRARY (Jamie Blandford); 71 AA PHOTO LIBRARY (Jamie Blandford); 72(t) SLIDEFILE; 72 b) SLIDEFILE; 73 AA PHOTO LIBRARY (Jamie Blandford); 74 AA PHOTO LIBRARY (Simon McBride); 74/75 AA PHOTO LIBRARY (Simon McBride); 75 SLIDEFILE; 76(t) AA PHOTO LIBRARY (Simon McBride); 76(bl) AA PHOTO LIBRARY (Simon McBride); 76 (br) AA PHOTO LIBRARY (Simon McBride)77(t) AA PHOTO LIBRARY (Simon McBride); 77(b) AA PHOTO LIBRARY (Derek Forss); 78/78 AA PHOTO LIBRARY (Simon McBride); 79(l) AA PHOTO LIBRARY Simon McBride; 79(r) AA PHOTO LIBRARY (Simon McBride); 80 AA PHOTO LIBRARY (Simon McBride); 80/81 AA PHOTO LIBRARY (Simon McBride); 81 AA PHOTO LIBRARY (Simon McBride); 82 AA PHOTO LIBRARY (Peter Zoeller); 82/83 SLIDEFILE; 83 SLIDEFILE; 84/85 AA PHOTO LIBRARY (Liam Blake); 86/87 AA PHOTO LIBRARY (Liam Blake); 87 AA PHOTO LIBRARY (Chris Coe); 88 AA PHOTO LIBRARY (Liam Blake); 88/9 SLIDEFILE; 89 AA PHOTO LIBRARY (LIAM BLAKE); 90 AA PHOTO LIBRARY (LIAM BLAKE); 90/91 SLIDEFILE; 91(r) Declan McGuire (Mayo News); 91(l) AA PHOTO LIBRARY (Michael Diggin); 92(t) AA PHOTO LIBRARY (Stephen Hill); 92(b) AA PHOTO LIBRARY (Stephen Hill); 92/93 SKYSCAN (John Eagle); 94 AA PHOTO LIBRARY (Simon McBride); 95(l) AA PHOTO LIBRARY (Simon McBride); 95(r) AA PHOTO LIBRARY (Simon McBride); 96(t) SLIDEFILE; 96 (b) SLIDEFILE; 97 AA PHOTO LIBRARY (Simon McBride); 98/99 AA PHOTO LIBRARY (Simon McBride); 99 BRUCE COLEMAN COLLECTION; 100/101 AA PHOTO LIBRARY (Chris Hill); 101(t) AA PHOTO LIBRARY (Chris Hill); 101(b) AA PHOTO LIBRARY (Derek Forss); 102/103 AA PHOTO LIBRARY (Simon McBride); 104(t) AA PHOTO LIBRARY (Michael Short); 104(b) AA PHOTO LIBRARY (Michael Short); 104/105 AA PHOTO LIBRARY (Michael Short); 106 AA PHOTO LIBRARY (Michael Short); 106/107 AA PHOTO LIBRARY (Liam Blake); 108(l) AA PHOTO LIBRARY (Simon McBride); 108(r) AA PHOTO LIBRARY Simon McBride; 109 AA PHOTO LIBRARY Simon McBride; 110 AA PHOTO LIBRARY (Chris Coe) 110/111 AA PHOTO LIBRARY (Simon McBride); 111 AA PHOTO LIBRARY (Michael Short); 112 AA PHOTO LIBRARY (Chris Hill); 112/113 AA PHOTO LIBRARY (Liam Blake); 113 AA PHOTO LIBRARY (Michael Diggin); 114/115 CHRISTOPHER HILL PHOTOGRAPHIC LIBRARY; 116/117 SLIDEFILE; 117 CHRISTOPHER HILL PHOTOGRAPHIC LIBRARY; 118/119 SLIDEFILE; 119 AA PHOTO LIBRARY (Chris Hill); 120(l) CHRISTOPHER HILL PHOTOGRAPHIC LIBRARY; 120(r) SLIDEFILE; 121 SLIDEFILE; 122 CHRISTOPHER HILL PHOTOGRAPHIC LIBRARY; 122/123 CHRISTOPHER HILL PHOTOGRAPHIC LIBRARY; 124 AA PHOTO LIBRARY (Chris Hill); 125(l) SLIDEFILE; 125(r) SLIDEFILE; 126 AA PHOTO LIBRARY (George Munday); 127(t) AA PHOTO LIBRARY (George Munday); 127(b) CHRISTOPHER HILL PHOTOGRAPHIC LIBRARY; 128 SLIDEFILE; 128/9 AA PHOTO LIBRARY (Michael Diggin); 129 AA PHOTO LIBRARY (Michael Diggin); 130/1 SLIDEFILE; 132/133 CHRISTOPHER HILL PHOTOGRAPHIC LIBRARY; 133(t) AA PHOTO LIBRARY (Derek Forss); 133(b) AA PHOTO LIBRARY (Chris Coe); 134 CHRISTOPHER HILL PHOTOGRAPHIC LIBRARY; 135(tl) CHRISTOPHER HILL PHOTOGRAPHIC LIBRARY; 135(tr) AA PHOTO LIBRARY (Chris Coe); 135(b) CHRISTOPHER HILL PHOTOGRAPHIC LIBRARY; 136 CHRISTOPHER HILL PHOTOGRAPHIC LIBRARY; 136/137 SLIDEFILE; 137; SLIDEFILE; 138/139 AA PHOTO LIBRARY (George Munday); 139 AA PHOTO LIBRARY (George Munday); 140 AA PHOTO LIBRARY (George Munday); 140/141 CHRISTOPHER HILL PHOTOGRAPHIC LIBRARY; 141(l) CHRISTOPHER HILL PHOTOGRAPHIC LIBRARY; 141(r) CHRISTOPHER HILL PHOTOGRAPHIC LIBRARY; 142 CHRISTOPHER HILL PHOTOGRAPHIC LIBRARY; 142/143 AA PHOTO LIBRARY (Chris Coe); 143(b) AA PHOTO LIBRARY (Chris Coe); 144 SLIDEFILE; 145(t) AA PHOTO LIBRARY (Chris Coe); 145(b) AA PHOTO LIBRARY (Chris Coe); 146 CHRISTOPHER HILL PHOTOGRAPHIC LIBRARY; 147(t) AA PHOTO LIBRARY (George Munday); 147(b) CHRISTOPHER HILL PHOTOGRAPHIC LIBRARY; 148/149 AA PHOTO LIBRARY (Chris Coe); 149(t) AA PHOTO LIBRARY (George Munday); 149(b) AA PHOTO LIBRARY (Chris Coe); 150(t) CHRISTOPHER HILL PHOTOGRAPHIC LIBRARY; 150(b) CHRISTOPHER HILL PHOTOGRAPHIC LIBRARY; 151 CHRISTOPHER HILL PHOTOGRAPHIC LIBRARY; 152(t) CHRISTOPHER HILL PHOTOGRAPHIC LIBRARY; 152(b) CHRISTOPHER HILL PHOTOGRAPHIC LIBRARY; 153 AA PHOTO LIBRARY (George Munday); 154/155 AA PHOTO LIBRARY (George Munday); 155 CHRISTOPHER HILL PHOTOGRAPHIC LIBRARY; 156/157 AA PHOTO LIBRARY (George Munday); 157 CHRISTOPHER HILL PHOTOGRAPHIC LIBRARY; 158 AA PHOTO LIBRARY (George Munday); 158/159 CHRISTOPHER HILL PHOTOGRAPHIC LIBRARY.

Gatefolds

Laytown: all photographs TREVOR JONES THOROUGHBRED PHOTOGRAPHY

Killarney: Peaceful waters near Killarney AA PHOTO LIBRARY(Simon McBride); Lough Leane AA PHOTO LIBRARY (Simon McBride);
Ladies View near Killarney AA PHOTO LIBRARY (Jamie Blandford); A stream tumbling through leafy oakwoods, Killarney AA PHOTO LIBRARY (Simon McBride); Climbing the steep Connor Pass near Dingle AA PHOTO LIBRARY (Jamie Blandford)

Galway International Oyster Festival: all photographs AA PHOTO LIBRARY (Simon McBride)

Belfast: The Crown Liquor Saloon, Belfast AA PHOTO LIBRARY (Chris Coe); River Lagan to Queen's and Queen Elizabeth II bridges CHRISTOPHER HILL PHOTOGRAPHIC LIBRARY; Looking northeast over the city at night CHRISTOPHER HILL PHOTOGRAPHIC LIBRARY; Dusk view over Belfast Lough CHRISTOPHER HILL PHOTOGRAPHIC LIBRARY; Sinking a pint of Ireland's favourite export AA PHOTO LIBRARY (Chris Coe)